DIY GARDEN PROJECTS

THE LiTTLe VEGGiE PATCH Co

To Emi and Marlowe,
for giving me kisses,
even when I have a beard.

THe LiTTLe VEGGiE PATCH co

DIY GARDEN PROJECTS

EASY ACTIVITIES FOR EDIBLE GARDENING AND BACKYARD FUN

MAT PEMBER
and **Dillon Seitchik-Reardon**

hardie grant books

CONTENTS

INTRODUCTION

At a point in your life – and it's hard to know when – the fear of not knowing something overwhelms the desire to learn. In an instant we're too afraid to ask questions, and every chance to learn is seen as a chance to fail. It's like we're sitting in the eternal classroom without the correct answer. Rather than curiosity satisfied by learning, the natural feeling is to curl up into a ball and roll away.

Inhibition is truly the greatest obstacle to learning, and we can be hampered by that feeling of reaching for something that's just beyond our grasp. Even as the reach extends further, with the gradual accumulation of skills and experience, the feeling continues to exist, if not grow. But somewhere along the line, excitement has joined the party. Now, in the pit of the stomach, there's an ever-present mix of both thrill and anxiety; it's a potent physiological cocktail that we've come to associate with being challenged.

Whereas once we were too afraid to step outside our comfort zone, we've come to accept that the first step towards developing skills is actually ignoring the fear of appearing unskilled and learning to cope with a lot of ugly mistakes. We all start out as absolute duds – let's not forget that our failures make the best stories. And we need a good story as much as we need those skills. Challenging yourself soon becomes contagious – a bit like eating hot chillies. What was once mostly a feeling of discomfort is now a sense that we're lifting our game, with a little discomfort thrown in on the side. There is no limit, only more to explore, so we keep experimenting and striving to create things. It seems only natural that we use the garden as our testing ground, growing food.

We can remember when we used to tie ropes like a four year old. We even put diesel in a petrol engine once. Never again. Seeing our old boss gulping on diesel as he siphoned it out of the tank made us determined not to make the same mistake twice. It's those catastrophic failures that will stick in the memory, lurking behind every petrol station refuel or picture frame hanging or light globe changeover. Fortunately, such stark failures have never deterred us – they actually encouraged a comeback.

Handiness isn't something you are born with, nor can you contract it like a virus. It's something that is learned, and we like to think there is nothing that we can't learn. For us that means the ability to do something well enough to enjoy it. Give yourself a break and let go of being the best. Only one person can be 'the best', but there is still a lot of room for the rest of us to have a little bit of knowledge. We will never be the best gardeners or cooks, but we sure do feel like studs every time we harvest some fresh basil or plant a fruit tree. We can now tie two knots as well as any sailor and we do it with the conviction of people who could know a lot more. That's really more than enough. Like most people, our journey to this point has been anything but linear. We never would have considered that one day we'd be teaching people how to make cubby houses or grow food.

However, we always did take special notice of the handy people in our lives. They seemed to be having so much fun tinkering with things, always building something new or siphoning diesel out of tanks. They seemed to have a healthiness and a spark in their eye. We would shake their thick, calloused hands and feel self-conscious about our own soft hands. So we bought some tools.

To my mom.
Obviously.

You'd be amazed at what can be made with a drill set, measuring tape and a circular saw. You'd probably be less amazed at how many things can also be made badly. We've measured a lot of things once and cut them at least twice. Projects have taken way too long or been terminated all together. We've dropped, lost or broken more than we care to think about. Mat has even managed to splinter his butt through thick cotton pants. But, somehow in the process, people have come to see us as 'handy'. Maybe it's because our hands aren't quite as soft anymore, or perhaps it's because our projects are always delaying others' plans.

Perhaps the hardest thing now is knowing when to stop, or recognising when the job's best left to others. Convincing yourself that a project is beyond you, or that the cubby house is actually finished, is like prematurely solving a mystery with the help of Google – it's just not natural. Now the ability to do stuff can severely limit your ability to stop doing things, and what was once the curse of soft hands is now the curse of giving everything a go. Need a lawyer? No. I can write a legal document. Plumber? We're constantly dealing with shit – how's this any different! Accountant? Bah humbug!

Today, there is the rise of the Jack of all trades – and I guess you can call us Jack – multi-tasking, multi-skilling, multi-jacking up things, too. But regardless of the outcome, the diversity in our skills brings great satisfaction and mystery, too. Who knows where new skills can lead? A half-finished aquaponics system or a new family business making natural icy poles? The unknown is the ongoing adventure.

So, as we have crafted our food-growing skills and developed swollen, calloused (some might say old Nonno) hands, so has the business. The Little Veggie Patch Co is our adventure and one that mirrors how we have evolved as people. It is what has led us here – to this book and to this series of projects. These will make you feel like both a stud and a dud, handy and useless – but, most importantly, they will encourage you to work at it some more. It's time to sharpen our collective teeth on these garden projects.

In *DIY Garden Projects*, we have chosen 38 of our favourite activities – those that put a sparkle in your eyes and a splinter in your butt – to help cultivate your handiness and develop a healthy attitude towards food. Each one is illustrated and easy to follow, and will give you a start on that ultimate compost set-up or seasonal seed guide. But given our history with refuelling, we'd never consider them definite. We're not really saying that our compost set-up is the ultimate compost set-up – it just feels ultimate to us and that's exactly the point.

Developing skills is all about giving it a go, and developing a healthy attitude to food is about giving it a go in the garden and all the places that surround it. So, whether in the backyard preparing your recycled planter box or in the kitchen tearing the place apart with the kids, let's abandon the anxiety and potential humiliation together and get a little excited. Remember, there is no limit, only more to explore, and we hope you start (or recommence) that journey with us.

– Mat and Dillon

PROJECT LIST

KIDS' GARDENING

My food experience as a kid was wholesome to say the least. Fresh produce from the patch, delicious fruit picked straight from the tree, lots of olive oil, cured meats and an early appreciation of table wine. It was an open invitation to food and customs both good and bad. But the food we ate was local and traditional, shaped by a culture with food as its epicentre for thousands of years.

Like all youth, I also had an intimate experience with fast food. McDonalds sponsored junior football programs across the country and incentivised goals with vouchers for cheeseburgers and fries. As a striker, and goals aplenty in under-7s, we often cashed them in on a Friday night. For a kid, this was party time. To say we were excited is an understatement – we went bonkers for Friday nights.

That fast food experience was reinvigorated in later years, once cheeseburgers and fries became a scientifically proven hangover suppressant. A routine of coming home from a big night out and drowning alcohol in fat was proven to have beneficial effects by some doctor, somewhere … I think. Either way, we lived by that credo for years.

What I realise now, as a parent, is how fine that balance must have been. My parents were strict but fair – letting us cash in our vouchers and taste wine at our Nonna and Nonno's dinner table, but digging their heels in when we turned feral, demanding more. It allowed us to make informed decisions in our adult lives, with cool heads, having had a taste of the good and the bad. So, finally, when we were let off the leash – free to roam wild – we developed our own habits based on a broad experience. Sure, we continued to eat crap through the years – we still do sometimes – but what we got was a balanced attitude towards food and lifestyle.

Healthy eating is just as much about experience as it is about the foods we put into our mouths. While we may turn to dieting and strict eating habits because our metabolisms have slowed down, the thought of kids dieting not only seems cruel, it seems to be food indoctrination!

The activities for your kids in this book are mostly about attitude, but a bit about eating, too. Let the little ones off the leash, let them roam wild and have some fun in and around the patch. There will be good and bad, successes and failures, but it will certainly help build a store of rich childhood

PROJECT DETAILS

TIME

DIFFICULTY RATING

BUDGET

THINGS YOU'LL NEED...

- 1 old strawberry or cherry tomato punnet
- 2 empty toilet rolls
- 1 sheet of newspaper (or scrap paper)
- seed raising mix
- seeds
- spray bottle

STRAWBERRY PUNNET GREENHOUSE

MINI GREENHOUSES FOR MINI PEOPLE

So much of our everyday rubbish can be reinvented into something useful. There is trash everywhere, begging you to let it realise its potential and help it find a second life. And that's useful on so many levels. Not only does that spare the immediate dump to landfill, but you also avoid buying something new, and that's a saving of resources all round.

Egg cartons and toilet rolls are two household waste products that we have previously converted into compostable seed pots, but have you ever looked at an old strawberry or cherry tomato punnet and thought 'Surely, that can be made useful'? Thankfully, someone did before us and that helped open our eyes to the possibility of converting these plastic tubs into mini greenhouses for the young ones. And, even better, they can be used to house your toilet roll seed pots.

As is so often the case, this is another example of a recycled material that seems almost readymade for its reinvented use. It has drainage holes in the bottom to allow drainage as required; durable, food-safe plastic to contain your seed raising mix; and a lid to allow you to open and then close the greenhouse, as conditions dictate.

The process is so simple, it is actually a tad embarrassing to label this a DIY activity, but I guess that makes it accessible to all children, from toddlers to teens.

1

Find a suitable **PLASTIC CONTAINER**. You want something that is relatively small, but has air holes in the lid. Strawberry or cherry tomato punnets are perfect for this project.

Cut each toilet roll in half so that there are now four little toilet rolls. These now become your propagation pots.

2 ›

Cut a square sheet of newspaper, or any scrap paper that is handy, so that it covers the floor of your **GREENHOUSE**, and place it at the bottom of the plastic tub.

‹ 3

››

4 ›

Place the propagation pots into the tub, sitting them on top of the newspaper. The purpose of the newspaper is to retain the small overflow of moisture and hold it within, making the greenhouse more **WATER-EFFICIENT.**

5

Fill each pot with seed raising mix, ready for the seed of your choice.

6 ›

Using the tip of your finger, make a small hole to the required depth for your seed. For the beans we are planting, this needs to be 20 mm (¾ in). Plant your seeds of choice, two in each hole in case one fails to germinate. Gently cover the seeds over with a sprinkle of the seed raising mix.

< 7 Give each of the pots a little water (enough to moisten the soil) and from this point forward, spray the whole inside of the greenhouse using a fan spray. The beauty of the strawberry punnet greenhouse is that it recycles the water already in it and your only job is to top it up every couple of days.

Leave watering to the **BOSS**.

< 8 Place the greenhouse somewhere that gets plenty of sunshine – perhaps on the kitchen windowsill. The kids will enjoy watching these little babies grow up. If the weather is particularly hot, open the lid and let them breathe. Otherwise, they will be happy **INCUBATING** in the cosy environment you created.

PROJECT DETAILS

TIME 🕐 🕐

DIFFICULTY RATING

BUDGET 💰 💰

THINGS YOU'LL NEED...

- fruit and veggies from the patch or fridge
- old seed packets
- oven
- assorted coloured oven-bake clay, such as Sculpey or Fimo
- cutlery (fork, knife, spoon)
- chopstick
- baking tray (cookie sheet)
- baking paper
- string or fishing line

CLAY FRUIT & VEGGIES
ARTISAN FOOD

Kids and clay are like tomatoes and mozzarella, like glitter and unicorns, like Ferraris and speeding tickets, like ... well ... I think you get the idea. The connection between kids and clay is undeniable. It is something intrinsic and fundamental that stirs from the deepest roots of our humanity. To create is to be human. To create something in the likeness of a fruit or vegetable ... well ... that is simply divine. So don't deny it – embrace it!

Like so many kids' projects, this is yet another chance to channel a known and loved activity into a broader conversation about what we like to eat. Food is a common thread that unites all people and perhaps the most important cornerstone of any culture. After all, food and eating are as much an emotional experience as a physical one. Unfortunately, many people have a story about how they were forced to eat [insert brassica of choice here] as a kid and have avoided it ever since. Playing games and crafting fruit and vegetables is the opposite of force-feeding Brussels sprouts. It is a successful method of building curiosity and excitement about different types of food.

There are, without a doubt, many products available at the local craft or art supply store, so don't stress over the brand. The important qualities are that the clay is non-toxic, can be baked in the oven and will not grow or shrink when it is hardened. The last is of particular importance because it allows you to bore holes through the fruit and vegetables, which can later be used to string them all together. As with an ex-punk with gauged ears, these holes should never close up. Clays are available in just about every colour known to man, but you can also start with white and paint the hardened clay once it's out of the oven.

1

Start in the veggie patch and identify what's in season. Ask the kids to try a bite of each fruit and vegetable and talk about how each one tastes.

2

HARVEST some of your favourite blue-ribbon fruit and veggies and bring them inside to be your still-life models. WATCH OUT KIDS - those are habanero chillies!

3

Go through the fridge and pick out a few more FAVOURITES. Now is a good time to prepare a couple of SNACKS to go along with this project! While you are inside, preheat the oven to the prescribed temperature - 130°C (275°F) if using Sculpey or Fimo.

< 4

Arrange some seed packets with your produce so that you have no shortage of **INSPIRATION**. The better the model, the better the sculpture.

Begin sculpting. Perhaps you subscribe to a post-impressionist nihilist abstract camp or are interested in synthesising the theoretical limits of the universe. At the Little Veggie Patch Co, we approach vegetables with a cacophony of temptation that is balanced by a traditional understanding of the moment.

5 >

6

Use some cutlery (or other kitchen utensils) to add texture to your mini clay replicas.

>>

< 7 Once you are satisfied with your **MASTERPIECE**, use a chopstick or skewer to punch a hole through some of the larger pieces. After they are baked, they will make excellent adornments to a fruit and veggie necklace.

8 Try adding a band of clay to the back of the sculpture to make a ring.

< 9 Place the sculptures on a baking tray lined with baking paper and fire the clay in the oven at the prescribed temperature and length of time (consult the baking instructions on the packet). Once they're ready, remove them from the oven and allow to cool before handling.

10

String up the necklaces and pop on those rings. There's nothing quite as fresh as premium fruit and veggie bling.

PROJECT DETAILS

TIME

DIFFICULTY RATING

BUDGET

THINGS YOU'LL NEED...

- zombie vegetables – carrots and spring onions
- lipped saucers
- water
- 100 mm (4 in) pots
- organic potting mix

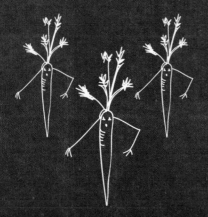

REGROWN PLANTS
VEGETABLE ZOMBIES BACK FROM THE DEAD

Any plant, no matter what variety, lives from its roots. Roots are its engine house – the motor that runs the rest of the body – and even when a plant concedes some loss of its foliage or fruit, either through harvest or neglect, a strong root system will enable the plant to spring back to life.

This allows us to regrow a number of different plants. If you hack a whole head of lettuce down to its stem, but ensure the roots remain intact, you'll be able to keep the plant alive through watering, and a new head of lettuce will surface. Similarly, when cutting spring onions down to ground level, the strong root zones left in the ground will help push out another perfectly good onion in no time, ready for harvest again. That all makes sense when the roots are left in the ground, intact, but what about those harvested and now out of the patch?

The world of root zombies is more one of fascination than fright. There are certain types of roots that can be treated carefully out of the ground and reintegrated back into the patch, bringing them back to productive life. This technique is useful for vegetables that need to be pulled out of the ground to be harvested – it can give them a second lease of life.

Root zombie resurrection, while being an activity of resourcefulness, is also a great eye-opener for kids on the biological make-up of our plants. It will show how plants can find ways to survive – even when the odds are stacked against them – and give some insight into how all plants need to be treated to not only survive, but to flourish.

‹1

First zombie off the rank, the carrot. Behold the little lifeless-looking zombies. More often than not, these will end up in the compost bin at best, but they can be **RESURRECTED AND REPLANTED** into the patch. This technique will also work for other root vegetables, such as beetroot, parsnip and turnips.

2 Find a lipped saucer and fill the base with water.

‹3

Trim the old carrot heads, if necessary, to roughly 1 cm (½ in) of the carrot root. Place the carrot tops in the water. The old sprouts should be above the water line.

»

Place the saucer and carrots in a **WARM SUNNY PLACE**, like on a windowsill. Remember, the carrots will be drinking the water to help promote growth, so keep topping it up as it is drunk. These zombies will re-sprout back to life in about ten days. They can then begin their second life in the patch.

< 4

Next zombie off the rank is the spring onion (though this also works well with leeks). In this case we're using leftovers from our market buy. However, if you are harvesting your own spring onions in your patch, remember to cut down the stem rather than pulling them out entirely. They'll regrow in the ground.

5 >

6

Spring onions are easier to **REVITALISE** than carrots. To start, fill up some 100 mm (4 in) pots with organic potting mix.

7

Now plant your spring onion — one in each pot — as though you were planting a stump seedling. Ensure that any root is sitting underground and the stem is sitting above ground, able to **BREATHE**.

8

Keep the spring onion well hydrated and in a matter of days the roots will **RETAKE**. Soon after that, you will notice a new shoot protruding from the stump. Frightening isn't it!

PROJECT DETAILS

TIME

DIFFICULTY RATING

BUDGET

THINGS YOU'LL NEED...

- herbs!
- nice sunny, in-ground space around the patch
- spade or garden fork
- compost
- organic slow-release fertiliser
- stepping stones/timber blocks for pathway
- pots for your mint (if using)
- plant labels
- water

SCENTED HERB PATHS
THE SMELL STUDIO

- - - 🪣 - - -

Nothing is better than seeing a child pick fresh herbs and attempt to sniff them with two-year-old nostrils. It's usually one of their first concerted efforts to use this sense and the evolution can be highly entertaining. Herbs are a no-brainer in a planting sense, but they can also double up as a studio for kids to develop their senses.

There's no doubt that these first attempts to smell are more an attempt to mimic the 'smell face' you show them. The little whiffs 'n' sniffs, along with the discovering eyes, can make you look pretty silly, but will show the capacity of your child to copy everything you do. Remember, your child is a sponge and is learning every moment.

While the first many attempts seem quite futile, only practice will get them in tune with their sense of smell, and that is when the discovering face takes on true meaning. That's when the scents start to be processed more internally and when the real discovery begins.

We have herbs littered around the yard that have become part of a pre-dinner ritual. My two little ones, Emi and Marlowe, will wander around the patches and grab, sniff and then ditch bits of mint, followed by sprigs of lemon thyme, followed by the mint again, and then occasionally a handful of the new rocket. The casualties of this routine are then tested by our dog, Molly, who is also developing her appreciation for culinary herbs.

This, of course, is a game that I started, so I have no right to correct it. Instead I take comfort that these sacrifices of the patch are the first meaningful part of an education.

1

Choose the herbs according to three considerations: they must work in a planting sense; they need to provide great insights for your kids; and they should be useful ingredients in the kitchen (it isn't just about the kids after all!).

Normally we like to elevate our patches and make them easier to tend, but that would be selfish wouldn't it? Ground-level herbs will be easier for the little ones to pick, and as they brush past and trample on them, they will arouse an **EXPLOSION OF SCENTS** that can also help mask any bad smells they may be generating.

2 >

< 3

Locate a nice sunny ground-level space for planting. Using your spade or garden fork, prepare the soil by spreading through some compost and organic slow-release fertiliser. Herbs will thrive in a **FERTILE**, free-draining soil, so preparation is key to ensuring planting success.

»

While you're going to **ENCOURAGE** your kids to venture through the herb patch, it's nice if you could provide a bit of direction rather than a random bush bash. Set out a path with stepping stones or timber blocks for the kids and the dog to follow.

‹ 4

We are all too aware of the stress involved when plants are young and there are kids around, so why take such a gamble? Herbs often come in a more mature form – in 200 mm (8 in) pots – and these larger plants will be much hardier, with a greater chance of survival.

5 ›

‹ 6

Organise the planting – perhaps keeping themes of herbs together, or colours, or not. All herbs tend to get along with each other so exact positioning should not matter too much. As a rule, keep mint in pots. Larger, taller herbs should sit further to the south and away from the path.

<7

Plant away. Get the little ones involved. This is also part of an **EDUCATION**, and hopefully they'll be of more help than hindrance ... And add some labels, so you don't forget what it is you've just planted!

8

Water in thoroughly. These guys will need water every day for the first month when establishing, but should then become pretty **SELF-SUFFICIENT**. It's best to plant in spring or summer.

PATCH FAVOURITE

PROJECT DETAILS

TIME

DIFFICULTY RATING

BUDGET

THINGS YOU'LL NEED...

- 1 x wooden box: 500 mm x 180 mm x 180 mm (1 ft 7½ in x 7 in x 7 in)
- drill set
- circular saw
- 1 x timber length: 1 m x 150 mm/20 mm (3 ft 3½ in x 6 in/¾ in)
- hammer
- 25 x 40 mm (1½ in) timber screws
- 10 empty toilet rolls
- 5 m (16 ft 5 in) of bamboo stakes
- paper (old magazines, waste paper destined for the compost bin)
- twigs
- 1 x timber length: 300 mm x 150 mm/50 mm (1 ft x 6 in/2 in)
- hot glue gun and glue sticks (optional)

BUG HOUSES
THERE GOES THE NEIGHBOURHOOD

Everyone has their own definition of a comfortable space and we all organise ourselves according to our own beat. Some of us go for high ceilings, wooden floors and no curtains, and others find comfort in a cave-like dwelling that is low-slung, dark and carpeted. These preferences become more interesting again when you live with others. Is butter a communal item? Will the common area be a Persian den of sin or an austere bastion of Swedish minimalism? Although sharing a space can often be a source of discomfort and passive aggressive ninjutsu, there's a lot to be said for cohabiting with a diverse group of people. The same can be said for insects in the garden.

There are all manner of insects in the veggie patch. Some of them are pests and some predators; some are metal heads and some are hippies. The point is that a veggie patch depends on a healthy ecosystem to thrive and that means a resident community of insects. As with any community, the difficulty is creating an environment in which everyone can come together.

Bug houses are a fun kids' activity and a great way to explore different shapes and textures, but also the kinds of insects they will attract. Beneficial insects pollinate, protect and break down organic matter in the patch, which makes the whole gardening experience a whole lot easier. Some insects are easy to lure in to your bug house – for example, a wall-mounted flat screen TV will attract bar flies, while perhaps the more practical quartered pine cone might be the perfect hideout for ladybugs.

The goal is to bring in as many of the beneficial insects as possible. Children should be encouraged to explore this mini-world and also keep the living arrangement current by performing the occasional renovation. Pay close attention to the seasonal changes in the bug house and if any numbers start to overwhelm the balance. Sometimes it may even be necessary to play Big Brother and remove an unpopular tenant

First up, drill holes in the back of the box. Next we need to compartmentalise the bug house into smaller condominiums. These will become the homes for each type of bug. As we value fairness, we will make each of these homes an equal size. So, if the wooden box has an internal measurement of 150 mm by 450 mm (6 in by 1 ft 5½ in), you'll need to cut two 150 mm (6 in) and three 140 mm (5½ in) lengths from our 150 mm/20 mm (6 in/¾ in) timber length.

‹ 1

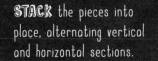

STACK the pieces into place, alternating vertical and horizontal sections.

2 ›

‹ 3

If your measurements were a little too good, you will find that it is quite a tight fit in the box. No worries — use a hammer to tap the wood into place.

‹ 4

Affix with a couple of screws on either side to hold them steady. Do your best and **DON'T FRET** too much about the integrity of the engineering and architecture.

Time to sort out the furniture. If you install one piece at a time, taking a moment to stand back and appreciate your work, and then repeating 150 times, it will take forever. Instead, prepare all the furniture at once. Collect your toilet rolls, cut up the bamboo, roll up bits of paper into tight tubes, and collect a pile of different thickness twigs. Some of these tasks are tailor-made for the kids, and the **TWIG MISSION** is one of them.

5 ›

6

One condo will become a purpose-built bee hangout, so we now need to cut one 140 mm (5½ in) slab from our 150 mm/50 mm (6 in/2 in) timber length.

‹ 7

Now, grab the drill and make a few different-sized holes in the surface of the slab. You will need some different-sized drill bits for this.

8

Place the slab in your compartment of choice and hold secure with a screw in one side. That should satisfy building standards. First unit sold!

‹ 9

Next, place the toilet rolls and the rolled-up paper. Though these can be stacked quite easily without glue, it's probably a good idea to secure the rolls with glue in anticipation of disruption to the building site, when the next **WAVE OF CONSTRUCTION** hits the bug house. Once again, let your own interpretation of the bug building standards be the guide here.

»

10

Repeat for the bamboo, **STACKING** up the layers and adding a squirt of glue if you fancy a little extra security.

11

Always wanted a room full of pine cones? Perfect!

12

Finish off with some twigs, straw, bamboo or whatever else is on hand.

13

With your bug house complete, find it pride of place among some **PRIME GARDEN REAL ESTATE.** Don't worry too much about finding the bugs – they will find you, enticed by your well-thought-out, well-constructed living spaces. You'll be surprised what types of little critters are attracted to the house.

FOR SALE

PROJECT DETAILS

TIME 🕐 🕐 🕐

DIFFICULTY RATING

BUDGET 💲 💲

THINGS YOU'LL NEED...

- large picture frame
- scissors
- heavy piece of poster board
- coloured cardboard or paper
- measuring tape or ruler
- pencils
- pens and textas (markers)
- paint
- old seed packets
- glue

Note: When you are planting seeds in the garden, try to remember to save the empty packets for this project.

SEASONAL SEED CHART

PUTTING THE ART BACK IN CHART

I think it was Shakespeare who once said, 'Does a winter tomato by any other name taste as sweet?' The answer is, of course, no. In making a cursory examination of a conventional supermarket, it is easy to forget that there are growing seasons for our fruit and veg. Tomatoes, for example, conveniently fill the aisles even in the heart of winter. Although we benefit greatly from hothouses and a range of growing climates, sometimes our food is simply, and certainly, out of season. One bite into a mealy, lifeless, sugarless and overly firm tomato makes this abundantly clear.

As an adult consumer, you eventually realise that this seasonality is also reflected in the price of produce. Sure, you can buy it, but there are market forces in place to remind you just how far that produce may have travelled to make it to your shopping basket. I love my winter avocados as much as the next guy, but it doesn't mean I don't fail to appreciate the freakiness of it. Children, on the other hand, may not pick up on the budgetary subtleties of our purchases, so a seasonal seed chart is a great way to make a tangible connection between what we eat and when we grow it.

A seasonal seed chart is that perfect place where garden, craft and kitchen intersect. While this is a fun craft project, most importantly, a seed chart is a way to prompt regular conversation about where food comes from. With very little guidance, it is amazing how much ownership kids will take of the patch and how quickly they start calling the shots.

1

Source a large picture frame. We have found some absolute gems at op-shops, but the choice is yours.

Cut a heavy piece of poster board to fit the frame. This will be the backdrop, so make sure it fits well.

2 ›

‹ 3

Using coloured cardboard or paper, divide the board into segments according to **SEASON** or **CLIMATE**. In milder climates we divide the board into warm, cool and year-around. In certain areas it makes more sense to divide the board according to the four seasons. In Melbourne we experience four seasons in a day, so we just go with what feels right.

››

Decorate the segments according to the mood and spirit of the season. Warm season, for example, may be brighter with **WARMER COLOURS**. Perhaps a beach scene or a cool drink. Holidays and leisure make a lot of sense. Kids often only require a slight prompt before they run away on a brilliant tangent.

〈 4

Move on to **DECORATE** another segment. Cool season will be represented with different colours and qualities. Autumn leaves, a cosy fire, winter sports, rainclouds or snow. Whatever embodies that season best within your family.

5 〉

Perennial plants are year-around and can take on an entirely different colour palette. Incorporate the bits and pieces that didn't make it into the other segments. Once you are satisfied with the styling, title the seasons in your most elaborate and decorative handwriting. Or, if your handwriting is like ours, avoid the embarrassment and learn from our mistakes – use a stencil.

〈 6

7

Hold on to those old seed packets, as they are the perfect material for this project.

Use glue to stick seed packets in their corresponding season. This is a great opportunity to discuss what kids like to eat. Start with the favourites and use the conversation to build interest in other veggies.

8 >

< 9

Mount the seed chart back in the picture frame. It will function not only as a fun piece of **ART**, but also as an ongoing guide to what to plant and when.

PROJECT DETAILS

TIME

DIFFICULTY RATING

BUDGET

THINGS YOU'LL NEED...

- small old esky container
- carpenter's square
- pencil
- jigsaw
- 300 mm x 300 mm (12 in x 12 in) sheet of 9 mm (⅜ in) plywood
- drill set
- 4 x 12 mm (⅜ in) screws
- 2 small hinge sets (screws included)
- 2 small latch sets (screws included)
- 2 pieces of clear perspex, 200 mm x 300 mm (8 in x 12 in)
- silicone glue
- bowl
- drill set
- 30-litre (27-quart) bag of premium quality compost
- water
- bag of 2000 worms (either tiger or red worms)
- food scraps

KIDS' WORM FARM
PETS WITH BENEFITS

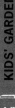

If a child could put a collar around a worm's neck and walk it down the street, they would. If a worm could talk, it would try to explain why that isn't such a good idea. But sometimes the relationship between child and pet doesn't make a lot of sense.

In our home, Molly the pooch gets dragged around by her collar and plonked down in the bathroom each morning to have her hair done with clips and bobby pins. Emi and Marlowe will then share their popcorn with her on the sofa, have a snooze in her bed and resume hostilities as they argue ownership of the fluffy toys they should all be sharing. But throw a worm in either of their hands and they'll drop Molly like a hot potato.

Kids' love of worms is more contagious than a rash at the local childcare centre, and it's a bond that is full of intrigue. Pet worms will introduce your child to the micro world of soil and all the life that surrounds it. Even as adults we perhaps struggle to understand just how vibrant that world is. Did you know that in a handful of soil there are more living organisms than there are people on Earth. That is the world the worm lives in, and introducing a worm farm to your kids will give them that chance to take an even closer look.

Using an old esky for the project helps give a new lease of life to an item that was destined for landfill, and is also perfectly insulated for lots of worm business. Most importantly, this project gives kids the opportunity to see worms at work, and to grasp the idea that a worm is not just a pet for playtime, but also a powerful garden ally.

1

Locate an old esky that never gets used. These things must breed when we aren't looking, as every year they seem to multiply in numbers.

»

Measure up a small rectangle from the esky, approximately 100 mm by 200 mm (4 in by 8 in). This is the trickiest part of the project, but also the most important, as it will be the **VIEWING GLASS**. Hopefully you will get the chance to see the worms while they're busy at work.

< 2

3

Use a jigsaw to cut out the window **OPENING**. You may need to drill one of the corners, just so that you can slip the saw blade in.

Because worms like to be **INSULATED**, they won't work where it's not dark and cosy, so the side openings will need to be shut up out of hours. To make a viewing door, take the outer layer of plastic and trace its shape onto a thin sheet of plywood.

< 4

‹5

Use a jigsaw to cut your plywood. Err on the side of too-small so that the door opens more easily. While the latch screws will help secure the plywood to the plastic door, it will need some reinforcement at the other end. Use a couple of 12 mm (½ in) screws in each corner to complete the job.

6

Mount the hinges to the plastic and ply door, using the screws from the hinge set.

‹7

The windows will no doubt need some help to shut tight, so attach a small, non-childproof latch that kids can easily use to keep them closed. This is tedious, **FIDDLY STUFF**, but will be worth it in the end.

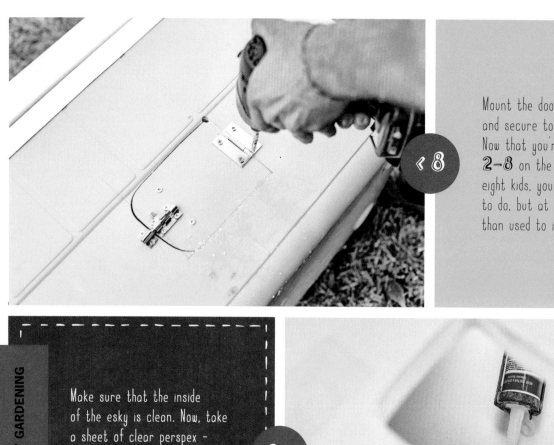

‹ 8

Mount the door hinge on to the esky and secure to the hardware. Great! Now that you're a pro, repeat steps **2–8** on the other side. If you have eight kids, you have a lot more work to do, but at least you are more than used to it.

Make sure that the inside of the esky is clean. Now, take a sheet of clear perspex – approximately 200 mm by 300 mm (8 in by 12 in) – and use silicone glue to attach it over the opening.

9 ›

10

Silicone takes a while to dry and will benefit from a bit of pressure, so try putting a brick or heavy book on top of the perspex until it is secure.

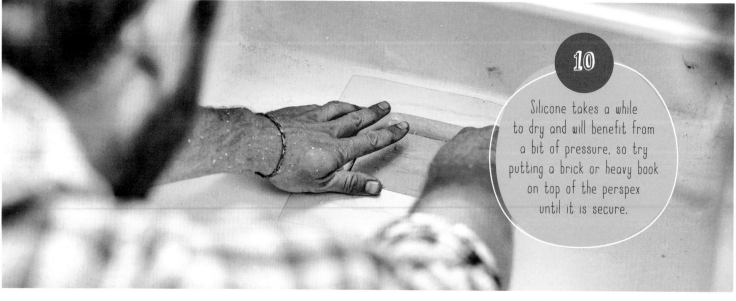

No worms yet, but these viewing windows are looking great.

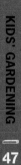

< 11

Place the esky on a small platform to elevate it so you can collect the **WORM WEE-WEE**. Place a receptacle (or wee-wee bowl) below the drainage valve (that has already been installed by a machine much craftier than you).

>>

‹ 12 Drill some small **BREATHING HOLES** – about twenty using an 8 mm (¼ in) drill bit – in the lid of the esky. Worms are like us and need air to work and play. Don't make them too large or the unit loses its insulation.

Throw in some **BEDDING** material (a bag of compost will do) and let your new pets settle in. This will all be a bit of a shock for the critters, so allow them a few days to get their affairs in order before putting them to work. Worms won't mind a little drink while they settle in and every week or so to keep them hydrated.

13 ›

14 We love a pet that earns its keep. While you are getting high-fives for your handiness, these guys will be converting your waste into beautiful soil.

After a couple of days, begin to feed the worms. Cut food scraps down to a size that they can more easily digest, and be careful not to overfeed them. Use your sense of **SMELL** to determine how they are progressing. If the farm is starting to smell a little funky, there's an anaerobic process occurring and the worms can't eat fast enough, so hold back. If it looks and smells like compost, the castings are ready for use in the garden, and the worms will happily take another serving!

Everyone can watch the worm world pass them by through the perspex peepholes. It's better than a window on the MS *Queen Elizabeth*.

PROJECT DETAILS

TIME

DIFFICULTY RATING

BUDGET

THINGS YOU'LL NEED...

- the craft of a fashionista
- old kids' clothing (shirt, pants, rain jacket, gloves, shoes)
- 2 small bamboo stakes
- 2 cable ties
- piece of hessian material
- straw
- soft twine
- a make-up kit, or a few fat textas (markers)

MINI SCARECROWS

SMALLER, CRAFTIER, BUT STILL DAMN SCARY ...

There are few activities in the patch that tick all the boxes, but scarecrow-making gives you the opportunity to grab a pen and paper, write a long list and then feel the sense of accomplishment as you tick a lot of stuff off. They help scare away pests; you can recycle your old clothes and reduce waste; you can get your handiness on and prove to all that your soft, callous-free office hands are totally capable of real work. And you can do all of this dressed up in your vintage 90s denims listening to Madonna. Tick, tick, tick, and tick.

While a scarecrow's effectiveness in scaring away birds and larger pests is often questioned, its effectiveness in bringing together generations is not. This is an activity that transcends age, and scarecrow-making will bring together the big and little kids alike.

Traditionally we have constructed larger, scarier, tall scare-monsters, but by scaling it down a little, your kids can make this project truly their own. They become the fashionistas of the project – and by using their old clothing, it helps strike an alliance between child and scarecrow that we, as adults, could never understand.

Nineties' horror movies have also proven that size does not always determine the degree of scariness, and even little plastic dolls can have an unlikely power and fear factor when put in the right context. Big scares have become so passé and the subtlety of a smaller, child-like scarecrow has a greater propensity to frighten. So don't see size as a limitation – see it as an opportunity to make truly freaky, truly scary, scare-monster creations.

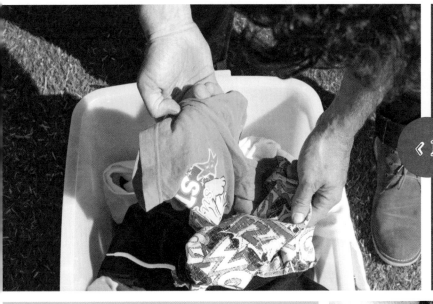

< 1

Go through your **KIDS' WARDROBE** and isolate the clothes that are available for this activity. Don't make the mistake of using the horrendous threads your Aunty Frances just gifted them if they are still a wearable size and she's due for a visit some day soon.

2 >

Start by constructing a small cross with the two bamboo pieces, held together with two cable ties. Tie one cable tie in one direction, and the second in the other. This may seem a complete waste of one perfectly good cable tie until you actually give it a go.

< 3

Next it's time to make the head, so grab your hessian and cut a piece approximately 500 mm by 500 mm (1 ft 7½ in by 1 ft 7½ in), which will sit underneath the top section of the cross.

>>

NOW GET STUFFIN'! Well, maybe not stuffin', but place a small amount of straw in the centre, bottom section of the hessian and then pull it over to form a straw hessian balloon. Don't over-inflate the scarecrow's head or you'll suffer the consequences. It just needs enough straw to form a ball that can be secured together.

< 4

5

Grab a length of twine and tie the neck that will hold the head and its contents in place.

The head's formed so now the bones of the body are ready for some meat. For the upper body, use a long-sleeved shirt, preferably a button-up. Slide it over the arm bones and begin stuffing life into the little monster. Things are starting to get a bit **FREAKY...**

< 6

7

In case of wet weather, a rain jacket is a good idea. Of course, we removed the sleeves because no fashion should be practical. Pull on some gloves.

8

Now, attach the legs to the torso. This is where it gets slightly **TECHNICAL**, because you'll need to cut a couple of small holes in the bottom of the shirt, so you can thread together the shirt and the pants, using the belt holes. Soft twine is best.

9

Resume stuffin'!
Fill up the pants and
then fine-tune your
work to date.

10 »

Now come the shoes. Make sure
the pants are bulky enough to
make the shoes a tight fit. That
way they'll stay on better.

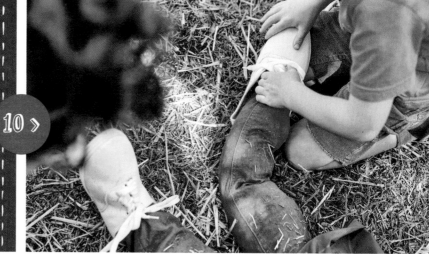

‹ 11

Time to raid the make-up kit
and give this **MONSTER** some
character. Eyeliner, lipstick,
a splash of Chanel No 5 ... or
alternatively use a few fat textas.

TOP 5

KID-FRIENDLY PLANTS TO GROW

Parents everywhere want their children more involved in the patch. But how do you break them into this world without having them break everything in their path? Everything you have spent so much time, energy and effort planting and caring for? Here are five plant varieties they can sharpen their teeth on by learning how to grow, drown, pull, obliterate and truly love them.

1 RADISHES

The radish is the 101 of gardening, even for kids, because growing it is child's play. By growing this vegetable, your children will receive an education on all the elements of growing food – and in a fast-paced, instantly gratifying fashion that is critical to keeping them interested. Shortly after sowing a radish seed (three or four days), that seed will germinate. And with the right level of care, little radish roots will be popping from the patch ready for harvest. Of course, not many kids will eat the radish, but if they can master this growing challenge, then as a parent it is your responsibility to master yours.

Growing carrots is all about the theatre of the harvest, and watching your child pull a carrot from the patch is an eye-opening experience for both of you. Everyone needs to understand that food comes in all shapes and sizes, not just the uniform standard found in the supermarkets. Pulling the gnarled, twisted, forked root from the ground highlights this fact and is the game we like to call vegetable lottery. An add-on to this game – perhaps a little premature for your little ones – is betting on the outcomes. How long will the carrot be? Will it be forked? Keep the wagers low so there's little to lose, but with certainty you are always going to gain a carrot.

2 CARROTS

③ MINT

Mint is an absolute no-brainer for the little ones. And thanks to its appreciation of water, it can become the crash test dummy for your kids. As we've quickly learned, a child's watering strategy is not too dissimilar to that of a cat trying to drown a rat, but at least mint gives kids the chance to learn watering techniques without bothering the plant too much. In fact, it will love them for it. We grow mint, not for this reason, but because we like to eat it. If we want to expand our mint, it's no more difficult than growing kikuyu grass. Just take a strand (root and all), bury it, water it and soon it will become the new kids' playground. However, it can quickly take over a garden bed, so consider growing it in a pot to keep it nicely contained.

This is an introduction to the rabbit food of the edible world — and like rabbits, lettuces are always plentiful. The beauty of lettuce is the way the plant is spurred on by harvesting. Taking the more mature, outer leaves will free up energy for the new generation to emerge, and this is a cycle that is looped until the plant turns bitter. Because you will often have too much in your patch, lettuce should be treated as the school of harvesting. So allow your kids to be kids — picking leaves, chunks, sometimes whole seedlings — and just be thankful they're not tending your black Russian tomatoes. If, by chance, the entire patch gets trashed, it's only a four-week wait, at any time of year, to build it up again.

④ LETTUCE

⑤ SUNFLOWERS

Who doesn't want to grow a sunflower? On our shelves, it's certainly the seed packet that attracts the most attention from the little ones. It seems that all kids have an affinity with tall, bright things, and what better way to satisfy this love than to grow sunflowers in the patch. Sunflowers love a hot, sun-drenched spot in the garden and will need plenty of room to move, but other than these space requirements, their demands are minimal. The beauty of the plant is the scale of its stalks and, of course, its flowering heads. This beautiful flower is a kid's friend for life, and will be nurtured and loved until its days are done.

PROJECT LIST

RE-CYCLING & UP-CYCLING

So much of our food journey is about anticipation and discovery. Growing, foraging and harvesting are unpredictable and uncertain, but there is joy in the process and an even greater excitement if you actually get something of value – even if it's only valuable to you. It's a feeling that comes from walking through a forest looking for mushrooms or patiently waiting for tomatoes to ripen. It's the thrill of casting out a fishing line and feeling a bite on the other end. We are hard-wired for the hunt and that's what recycled materials are all about.

Some of our favourite jobs have been working with clients who didn't want anything new. We have planted a 30-year-old tree in a giant cement mixer; built wall gardens from metal sultana bins; and turned a shipping container into a café. And, obviously, we think that apple crates can become just about anything. In all of these cases, we didn't know where the hunt was going to lead, and it was only after finding the right material that its purpose became apparent.

We don't want to give anyone the wrong impression – salvaging isn't a glamorous pursuit. There's a danger in that once you see the value in one thing, you will start to see the value in every single piece of junk out there. Before you know it you are sleeping in a chair because your bed is full of cable drums. The trick is knowing what kind of relationship you want. You simply can't bring every great idea home. Get out there and have a few flings. Gain some experience so that you can be more certain about the good ones. There will be greasy handshakes and staffies lounging in the sun. There will be splinters and rusted nails. There will be so many bad ideas. But there will also be cement mixers full of trees, and that is what you do it for.

At its core, this chapter is not about a few specific ideas that everyone will follow, it is about getting people excited to go outside and find their own treasure. It is about exploring new places and challenging yourself to be creative. The more we play with upcycled materials, the more possibilities we see. Ideas build on ideas. In providing some examples, we hope that people will realise how much potential exists, which is something we are only now realising ourselves.

PROJECT DETAILS

TIME

DIFFICULTY RATING

BUDGET

THINGS YOU'LL NEED...

- recycled packing crate
- castors (swivelling wheels)
- 20 x 50 mm (2 in) bulge head screws
- drill set
- food-safe plastic (builders film)
- timber for bracing (optional)
- old plastic pots
- styrofoam boxes
- weed matting
- staple gun and staples
- 5–10 x 30-litre (27-quart) bags of premium organic potting mix (depending on the size of your container)
- your favourite herbs or other plants

SALVAGED RAISED PLANTER BOX
ONE MAN'S TRASH

People now seem to talk about raised garden beds with an overwhelming belief they will make expert gardeners of them. However, the sad truth remains that if you are a delinquent gardener and kill plants unwittingly, a raised bed won't stop this happening – though it will make it much harder.

A raised garden bed can be anything that is used to elevate the growing level of your garden and it doesn't have to be built for that purpose. In fact, a number of salvaged items can be used to fulfil the need. This means a treasure hunt and the search for useful things that cost little to no money.

When searching for inspiration, choose from materials that are non-toxic. After all, one of the motivations of growing your own produce is to ensure the food grown is chemical-free and damn tasty, so why compromise that by using a vessel that could leach nasty chemicals?

Practise your haggling well before you are called into action at whatever salvage yard, refuse centre or hoarders' house you stumble across. Our technique is the three-phase strategy – start low, look confused and don't say another word. We've had mixed success over the years. It's a bit like fishing – you often don't even get a bite, but in the right conditions and at the right time, you could be in for a haul.

Remember that traditional raised garden beds are generally built out of durable materials to last and on soft landscapes so that water will drain through the existing soil structure. Our salvaged or upcycled items – fruit bins, packing crates, wheelbarrows, old bath tubs – are contained and, in some cases, less than durable. They are guided by a different set of rules for preparing them and ensuring they function well.

1

First comes the **HUNT**. If you're anything like us, you will relish the challenge of finding your recycled crate and at a rock bottom price. Without giving too many of our secrets away, look up timber recycling centres or maybe you know an importer. Tiles, car parts, white goods, garden pots, things used to disguise illicit drugs – all sorts of interesting stuff – arrive on boats in nice, big wooden boxes. When **SCOUTING**, make sure you don't turn up in an expensive 4x4 (SUV); it will knock you back a step in the haggling process.

Because your raised bed is contained, it has the potential to be **MOBILE**, and castors will help with this. However, be aware that a large box filled with wet soil is really, really, really heavy and will not only require heavy-duty castors but also a smooth rolling surface. Turn the container upside down and attach each castor to each corner using hex screws. It's best to drill a leader hole before attaching each screw, and an impact drill will make the job a pleasure.

‹ 2

The next thing to consider is **DRAINAGE**. Even though the recycled crates you use won't be watertight, they won't drain particularly well, so be generous in adding drainage holes using the power drill and some 10-20 mm (½-¾ in) drill bits. A couple of tiny holes at the base generally won't be sufficient - give water freedom and help it out.

3 ›

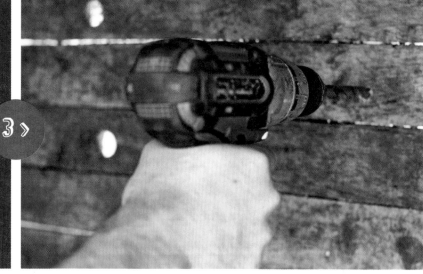

Be aware that there will be drainage **RUNOFF**, so be mindful of where the water will run when placing your box. Locate it close to a drainage point or near soft landscaping (grass, for example). This will mean your space will be left clean and dry rather than a slippery, dirty mess.

‹ 4

‹ 5

Unlike your traditional raised bed that is built to last (made out of lovely dense timber or stone), your recycled unit was probably not designed to hold large quantities of wet soil. When you can, help **PROTECT** the wood from premature rotting by lining the box with a food-safe plastic. Cover and staple the sides because they will make contact with wet soil but don't line the base and make it watertight again!

With a deep unit, decide whether to entirely fill it with soil. If you are planting a fruit tree, this may be necessary, in which case it is best to **BRACE** your crate. Do this by attaching two timber panels on the inside wall of the crate and then joining them with a bracing timber. This way the force that the soil and water put on the unit is largely diminished.

6 ›

‹ 7

Most edibles, however, only require 300 mm (12 in) of soil, and reducing the volume will lessen the stress on the container. You can build a false bottom using old plastic pots, covered over with styrofoam boxes for extra strength. This will elevate the soil height. First, build your pots up. Once you are satisfied with the level of the pots, place styrofoam boxes upside down over the top, which will create a relatively even, flat base.

››

‹8 Now, lay weed matting over the top and staple it into the timber so that the soil does not fall through.

Fill with **GOOD-QUALITY** organic potting mix. Don't be stingy at this point. In small spaces, better quality soil makes all the difference.

9›

10 Plant out with seasonal produce.

PROJECT DETAILS

68

TIME

DIFFICULTY RATING

BUDGET

THINGS YOU'LL NEED...

- 1 x 2-litre (68 fl oz/8 cup) empty milk bottle with lid
- permanent marker
- scissors
- old cotton t-shirt
- domestic stapler and staples
- premium organic potting mix
- seedling of choice

POTTING MIX

SELF-WATERING MILK CONTAINER

GOT MILK?

I never really came to grips with the scale of the dairy industry until I had kids. Within a couple of years my partner gave birth to two beautiful little girls and before we knew it, both of them turned into milk monsters.

Milk is everything for a milk monster. It is their mornings, their nights, their middle of the nights and, when in doubt, it is any other time of day they start misbehaving and tearing the place apart. I still don't feel completely comfortable that my children's main source of nourishment comes from a farm animal that goes moo, but I am comfortable and confident that I am now truly a parent. We now duly pay taxes and contribute to the economy because our kids drink most of our income in milk.

Rather than live in fear at the idea of an empty bottle of milk when the monsters are calling, shift your focus to creating a handy planting device, because a bottle can be easily converted into a self-watering planter. A planter that waters itself you say?! Yes, it is possible to build a mini wicking planter using nothing more than an old milk container and some simple household materials.

This could be the beginning of the end of the milk horror story, and the time you start feeding the monsters more vegetables instead.

1

Cut the plastic milk bottle horizontally about a third of the way down, just underneath the handle. You want this to be even, so rather than free-styling it, make a line and follow it.

2

Great start. The top section that has the handle will be flipped upside-down to become the planting section, and the bottom part of the bottle is now the water reservoir.

3

Fill the reservoir with about 30 mm (1¼ in) of water.

Grab your old cotton t-shirt. It's time to create your 'wick', which will help pull the water from the reservoir to the soil where your seedling will use it. Have you ever dipped a tissue in a glass of water and watched the water travel vertically through the fabric? That's what your cloth will do, too. Cut a 20 mm x 100 mm (¾ in x 4 in) strip from your t-shirt.

< 4

5

Push the wick through the bottom of the planter – where the lid once was – leaving half of it **DANGLING**.

< 6

Staple the top of the wick using a conventional office or domestic stapler. This will keep it from slipping.

7

Cut a cross into the lid.

8 ›

Feed the wick through the lid and screw it back onto the milk bottle. This will allow the wick to **DRAW WATER** up into the planter, while the cap will prevent soil from falling into the reservoir.

‹ 9

Transformation is nearly complete. Now, combine the two sections to create the Optimus Prime of small space gardening.

‹ 10

Fill up the planter with premium organic potting mix. You know, the good stuff. The stuff that **SMELLS LIKE DARK CHOCOLATE.**

11

Now, take your seedling of choice and plant it into your soil. Ideally you want a plant that can mature in this small space, such as a variety of lettuce or a basil plant. Water it in so that the soil is damp. The wick will draw water from the reservoir below and replenish the plant as required. Top up from time to time or as the water level drops.

PROJECT DETAILS

TIME

DIFFICULTY RATING

BUDGET

THINGS YOU'LL NEED...

- selection of spoons
- vice
- 2 wood blocks (offcuts), larger than the spoons
- alphabet metal stamps (can be purchased online)
- hammer

Note: In the absence of a vice, spoons can also be flattened by sandwiching them between two pieces of hard wood and parking a car on top.

RECYCLED SPOON MARKERS
SPOON ME

Everyone has had that experience at a contemporary art exhibition when you think, 'Huh ... I could do that. Why didn't I think of that?' I don't say this to diminish or undermine the artistic merit of hanging a pink string from the ceiling or painting a single black circle on white canvas. The genius is, of course, having the idea in the first place. Such was my experience at a boutique gardening shop when I first encountered recycled spoon markers. It is a simple and practical use of an everyday item, and yet it never occurred to me. Unlike the canvasses with badly painted geometric shapes that remain hidden in my garage, the recycled spoon marker is one case of artistic inspiration that I don't mind sharing with the world.

While it can be fun to leave your patch unmarked, having a few signposts along the road makes navigation a lot easier. And, after all, who doesn't like a good spoon? Unlike the plastic tags that come with a punnet of seedlings or faded popsicle (ice lolly) sticks that won't make it through the season, the recycled spoon marker will be an enduring monument to your handiness and commitment to gardening.

Selection is half the fun. Go through that cluttered kitchen drawer and assess what actually gets used. Perhaps that clam-shaped spoon that infuses every bite with a metallic taste would be better off in the garden. Maybe the spoon that bends in half when plunged into a tub of ice cream has been trying to tell you something all along. Whether you consider yourself a big spoon or a little spoon, we all know that a wide range of shapes and sizes will make for a much more interesting gardening landscape.

1 Find and assemble a collection of spoons. If you are in a share house with only four spoons in the drawer, do your housemates a favour and wander down to the Salvation Army for additional supplies.

2 First, you need a **VICE**. By this we mean a metal tool with moveable jaws, typically attached to a workbench.

3 Use the two wooden blocks as a sort of sandwich for your spoon, which will allow for a much more even distribution of force across the whole spoon. Any short offcuts of wood should do the trick, provided that they are larger than the spoon head in question. Hardwood is best, as softer woods will dent under pressure.

»

4

If it's too difficult to hold it all together, ask a friend for a helping hand. It's good to get other people involved and will bring you closer together.

Slowly clamp the vice shut. This may take a bit of force and is a great opportunity to demonstrate your fitness. Roll up your sleeves and take it slowly, lest you have any workplace accidents.

5 ›

‹ 6

Once you feel you have sufficiently flattened the spoon and impressed your friend with your Herculean strength, loosen the vice and check your work.

If the head of the spoon is completely flattened it will make the letter stamping a lot easier. Feel free to repeat the clamping process until you are satisfied.

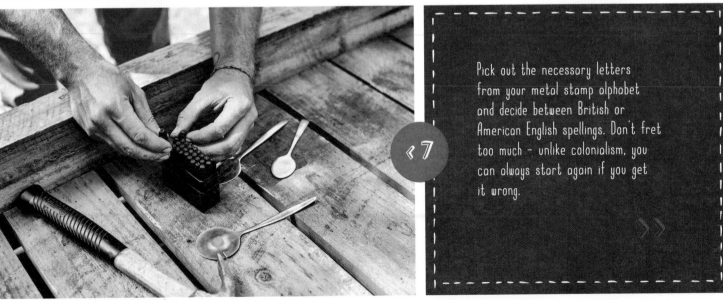

《7

Pick out the necessary letters from your metal stamp alphabet and decide between British or American English spellings. Don't fret too much – unlike colonialism, you can always start again if you get it wrong.

》》

‹ 8

Carefully hammer the metal stamps into the spoon, being mindful that a poor strike can send the metal stamp flying into oblivion and result in an unsightly black thumbnail. We are trying to be **GREEN THUMBS** here, mate.

Take a moment here. You have just created an object of pure **BEAUTY**. The European masters would be proud. Vincent van Spoon, eat your heart out.

9

Way to go! Locate the corresponding plants in the garden and give them a marker to be **PROUD** of. These markers will last much longer than the plants themselves, so store them away during the off-season and bring them out with each year's fresh crop.

PATCH FAVOURITE

PROJECT DETAILS

TIME

DIFFICULTY RATING

BUDGET

THINGS YOU'LL NEED...

- at least 1 free weekend
- 4 recycled apple crates (in good condition)
- reciprocating saw
- drill set
- 50 x 40 mm (1½ in) timber screws
- jigsaw
- 1 length of pine timber: 1.2 m x 70 mm/ 35 mm (3 ft 11 in x 2¾ in/1½ in)
- 10 x 70 mm (2¾ in) bulge head screws
- small wooden ladder
- circular saw
- 1.2 m x 1.2 m (3 ft 11 in x 3 ft 11 in) marine-grade plywood
- fake grass offcuts

THE APPLE CRATE CUBBY HOUSE

HOW TO WIN PARENT OF THE YEAR

The thing I've learnt most by being a parent is that your children give you the permission slip to do stuff – stuff that you didn't have the skills or resources to do as a child. Like eating cake for breakfast. Or driving a full-scale excavator. Or spending a month of weekends building the best cubby house of all time.

While there are some things you do purely for your kids, there are others that are more about team us – and building a cubby house that makes the family home look like the second dwelling will help infuse happiness into everyone's life. Since building my first dream cubby house, I've taken praise from my partner, my kids, my parents and my next-door neighbour, Paul. I am now the perfect partner, father and son, and I know that Paul is totally disgusted with me.

The real difficulty with large, handy projects is knowing when to draw the line and decide that enough is enough. Some people have the tendency to always need to evolve or improve, and the dream cubby house has the potential to starve you of time and money while feeding that affliction.

A cut-off size for this project is as big as possible without needing planning approval. But to make this achievable for people who don't love their kids as much as I do, we've scaled it back a few steps so you can manage it over a weekend.

Much like the humble pallet, there are 99 uses for an old apple crate and this cubby house is yet another one.

1

Make space for the **DREAM** cubby house. You'll need 1.22 m by 1.22 m (4 ft by 4 ft) at ground level for the structure itself, and enough room at the front for a comfortable entrance. The cubby will be approximately 2 m (6 ft 6½ in) in height.

◄2

Cut down one of the apple crates for spare timber, which will come in handy throughout this project. Because the crates have been ageing and the nails rusting, it's hard to pull them apart with a hammer and jimmy bar. A reciprocating saw is a pretty essential tool. Don't worry if a few timber panels snap or crumble along the way. You will only need about half the panels and braces – the rest will be excellent kindling!

3

Place one crate level on the ground and another upside down over the top. Done! The dream cubby house is complete! Ah ok, not quite.

< 4

First, make the doorway. It's best to **BRACE** the door to the size you want it before cutting out the panels. Without support, the timber will fall on your saw blade as you're cutting, and you'll be spending more time forking out change to the swear jar than building the cubby. Use some spare timber panels to construct the framework for the door, attaching with 40 mm (1½ in) timber screws.

< 5

Now, cut the door out following the edges of the doorframe you have installed. Presto! Door installed, and the perfect entrance to a dark, wooden box.

With the door installed, the place will need a couple of windows – one on either side. Follow the same technique by bracing the window with more spare timber panels cut to size. Make your window frames four panels in height and 800 mm (2 ft 7½ in) wide.

6 >>

7

Now, cut out the panels and your windows are nearly complete.

>>

‹ 8

These offcuts can be used for a bit of finishing around the window. One piece will form the windowsill from which the kids can serve tea and cupcakes. Attach this windowsill using 40 mm (1½ in) timber screws.

< 9

The other panel can form a little bit of eave to protect the tea and cupcakes from the weather. Once again, attach using screws.

10

You might want to take this opportunity to carpet out the interior with some lovely fake grass. Just a thought!

< 11

Cut off the legs and centre-brace of the upside-down crate that is currently making the roof. This is easy enough with the right tools – we use a reciprocating saw with a flexible blade to cut the legs free.

13

This wouldn't be the **DREAM** cubby house without a second level to take in the city views, so there's still more than half the house to complete. Now we call upon the last crate, but first we need to cut off its legs and centre braces. Installation of the second level is now straightforward. Just put the cannons to work and lift it into place, open-side up. **POW! SUCH TOUGH GUYS!**

14

Next up, make the top level feel part of the home by **REINFORCING** with 40 mm (1½ in) screws that pull the timbers together and make them one.

It's structural time! For the top level to be accessible it will need a ladder entrance up through the floor. First, reinforce the floor where it will soon be weakened by your cuts using the 1.2 m by 70 mm/35 mm (3 ft 11 in by 2¾ in/1½ in) pine. This piece should be secured far enough away from the building edge so the ladder will fit in the opening you're about to create. Use at least half a dozen 70 mm (2¾ in) bulge head screws along the timber length.

15 ›

16

Also insert horizontal screws through the sides of the cubby house into the end of the pine length.

17

Now, cut out three sections of panel along the timber brace.

18

Loosen the pieces free to reveal the ladder hole.

‹ 19

Put your ladder into position. **CONGRATULATIONS** – the kids now have access to a rooftop alfresco dining area (people pay top dollar for those spaces!). Of course, no responsible parents will be happy if their children spend time in the weather and catch themselves a cold, so it's probably best to make it (relatively) waterproof.

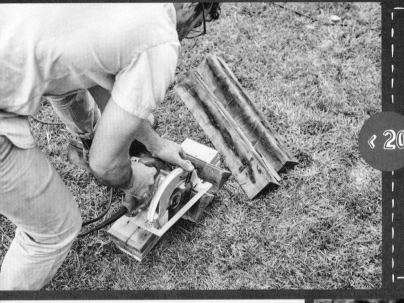

‹ 20 To hold the immense weight of the roof (the thin sheet of marine-grade plywood), you will need to construct some uprights. For **AESTHETIC** purposes, we use old corner braces from the crate we cut down. Leave two at their full size (one end trimmed on a slight 20° angle) and trim the other two down to 500 mm (1 ft 7½ in), cutting them on a slight angle.

Attach a 600 mm (1 ft 11½ in) length of timber in each corner, leaving half standing above the current structure. Our roof braces will be attached to these. **21 ›**

‹ 22 Place the two full-corner braces at the front and the smaller pieces towards the back, using the timber panels to hold them together.

23

Finally, attach the roof with a screw in each corner and the shell is built.

24

Using what's left of the spare timber, clad the roofing uprights and roof join for a neater finish.

25

All that's left to do is **DECORATE** the interior and exterior and then invite over your parents, the in-laws, neighbours, friends – in fact anyone who you love to hear kind words from – and bask in the glory of being a great person.

PROJECT DETAILS

TIME

DIFFICULTY RATING

BUDGET

THINGS YOU'LL NEED...

- 1 pallet
- handsaw
- reciprocating saw
- measuring tape
- 25 x 40 mm (1½ in) timber screws
- drill set
- sandpaper and wooden block or electric sander
- 4 x small hooks
- 2 x Y-brackets
- 2 x medium-sized funnels (preferably metal)
- old metal rake head
- 2 x L-brackets
- spirit level
- 2 x 50 mm (2 in) bulge head screws

THE ULTIMATE TOOL SHED

SHE'S ALL THAT

You can gain a lot of insight into a person by visiting their home. Do they make their bed or do they spoon a giant pile of laundry every night? Are they playing dish Jenga or does the multi-purpose surface cleaner come out after every meal? Are they reading *50 Shades of Grey* or *The Picture of Dorian Gray*? Fairly or not, these tiny observations make an impression. The same can be said of the garden, which often manifests in various states of organisation or neglect.

While I cannot speak for messy people, I can say that my own mind is messy enough and that I need a tidy space to stay focused. Cleaning something helps me to gain more respect and better appreciate that space. After cleaning my car, for example, it often feels like it drives better. Sometimes a little maintenance is all that is required to see the potential in something. Building a nice tool shed is the same, in that it can help you to see your garden differently. Some would say, through rose-coloured glasses.

The ultimate tool shed is a way to show your style and take some pride in the garden. The reality is that for us small-space gardeners, we don't need that many tools. A couple of little hand tools, twine, gloves and maybe some natural pest control is plenty. It is mostly a question of consolidating and refining what you already have – much like the classic American teen movie *She's all that*, in which the main character is seen as a geeky loser until she ditches her paint-covered overalls and dorky glasses. A slight change can totally shift your perspective, only in this case building a tool shed will help you to get more out of your garden, not go to senior prom with Freddie Prinze Junior.

Find a **HANDSOME PALLET**. Not just any one will do. I'm talking about something that will only get better with age. You are looking for the Robert Redford of pallets.

»

2 Use a handsaw to cut off one section of the pallet (two timber panels wide). This will be used as scrap timber for the rest of this project.

3 Use a reciprocating saw to strip down the pallet offcut.

4 Next it's time to make a single shelf for the middle row. Measure the gaps in between pallet sections. They will be a little bit less than half the width of the pallet.

5

Use a handsaw to cut the scrap timber down to size. These will fit either side of the central spine.

Use 40 mm (1½ in) screws to attach the newly cut lengths to the bottom of the shelf, thus creating a proper platform for the middle section. This will be a **MULTIPURPOSE STORAGE SPACE** for things like plant fertiliser, pest control and seeds.

6 ›

‹ 7

Now that you have made all of your cuts, sand back the pallet until smooth, taking care to eliminate any splinters. Wrapping the sandpaper around a wooden block will make this process **FASTER AND EASIER**. Using an electric sander will make it even faster and easier again.

››

8

Fix some small hooks on the inside of the uppermost section of the pallet. These will be great for hanging small tools.

Screw in a couple of Y-brackets at the bottom of the tool shed. These will be useful for holding medium-sized tools such as a short-handled shovel or mattock.

9

10

Attach the two funnels to the pallet using a couple of short screws. Feeding twine through a funnel makes it much easier to cut and **ELIMINATES** annoying tangles.

We found this old rake head lying around and it already had a hole from which it would have connected to the handle. If you can find something similar, use a screw to **MOUNT IT** to the tool shed. It's another useful (and decorative) hanger for tools.

< **11**

12

Attach a couple of L-brackets on either side of the tool shed.

MEASURE the height of your longest tool. This will determine how high the pallet is hung.

< **13**

14

Lift the pallet and use a spirit level to help set it up just right.

15

Mount the tool shed to the wall using 50 mm (2 in) bulge head screws.

< 16

Why not hang a few more hooks underneath the centre shelf? This just means that you will have more room for your tools.

PROJECT DETAILS

- - - - - - - - - - - - - - -

TIME 🕐 🕐

- - - - - - - - - - - - - - -

DIFFICULTY RATING

- - - - - - - - - - - - - - -

BUDGET

- - - - - - - - - - - - - - -

THINGS YOU'LL NEED...

- - - - - - - - - - - - - - -

- cable drum
- circular saw
- sander
- rocks, scoria, offcuts, broken pots
- premium potting mix
- herbs and veggies of your choice
- water

POTTING MIX

CABLE DRUM TABLE PLANTER

READYMADE RECYCLED PRODUCTS

Coming in third of the all-time most versatile recycled products is the cable drum. While its circular nature makes it less applicable to constructions than the pallet or fruit crate, one advantage over its counterparts is that it can be easily transported without machinery or a motor vehicle. And when you have finished rolling it to its resting place, simply tip it onto its side to convert it into a readymade table.

The first time I sat at a cable drum table it felt like I was sitting at an art installation. Pieced together with such intricacy, it was surely designed by someone who not only appreciated cable, but also had an aesthetic flair. And I couldn't help but feel the value of the unit outweighed the value of what it was designed to carry, and that made me feel uneasy.

As with most things old and beautiful, they have gradually been replaced by something new and plastic. The wooden wheels, which will always be considered nothing less than works of art, have been phased out in favour of efficient and cost-effective plastics. But the durability of the wooden devices mean a lot are still in circulation today, being flogged off by wise guys who recognise things of value.

If you do your research you can come across cable drum cities – stacks of different-sized and coloured wheels – where, for a price, you can purchase the drum of your dreams. Perhaps before forking out cash on a cable drum for this activity, call around to some wiring wholesalers and see if you can intercept one before the wise guys come for collection.

‹ 1

Hunt down and secure the services of a lovely, wooden cable drum. For the purpose of a table, it'll need to be approximately 800–900 mm (2 ft 7½ in–2 ft 11½ in) in height when laid on its side. Anything smaller can be made into the kids' table.

To avoid constantly hitting the base of the drum as you try to tuck in your chair, you need to trim this with a circular saw. Flip it over and make it a square large enough to **SUPPORT** the weight of the table. In this case, we cut it down to a 500 mm by 500 mm (1 ft 7½ in by 1 ft 7½ in) square base.

2 ›

3

Some cable drums will have a hole in the centre, which makes planting simple. Our drum didn't, so we used a circular saw to cut an opening in the top.

Any cable drum worth its salt will have more than a few splinters waiting to embed themselves in your delicate skin. Take a sander to it and with a little work the wood should look and feel **REJUVENATED**. A little sanding will also make the wood more receptive if you want to cover it in varnish, which will then help protect the table from the weather.

‹ 4

Fill the cable drum with a premium potting mix. Bear in mind that many plants don't need much more than 300 mm (12 in) of soil to grow. So, feel free to chuck in some rocks, scoria, wooden offcuts or anything else that can fill the space and raise the planting level.

5 ›

‹ 6

Plant the herbs and veggies of your choice. We find that something **LOW MAINTENANCE** and perennial is best. Give the plants a good watering in.

TIME

DIFFICULTY RATING

BUDGET

THINGS YOU'LL NEED...

- storage container
- 90 mm (3½ in) PVC pipe with cap
- pencil
- handsaw
- drill set
- 90 mm (3½ in) PVC elbow
- measuring tape
- silicone glue
- 25 mm (1 in) PVC valve fitting
- expanded clay or scoria
- Geotech fabric (or weed mat)
- scissors
- premium organic potting mix
- favourite plants
- water

STORAGE CONTAINER WICKING BED

GARDENING FOR TRANSIENTS

As a home renter, two ideas weigh heavily on my domestic decisions. The first is making sure that I don't accumulate too many things. I know that with every move, I will have to perform a large cull of my possessions. This is not necessarily a bad thing and in some ways can even be cathartic, like giving away an ex-girlfriend's wetsuit or bringing unused clothing to an op shop. Nevertheless, I try not to acquire too much in the first place so as to avoid any future conflict.

The second renter's dilemma is how much work to put into the property. Sure, it is great to be able to hang pictures willy-nilly and put holes in someone else's walls. However, it is not as much fun to pour years of time and energy into a garden, only to move out and abandon it to ambivalent new caretakers.

The storage container wicking bed is a way to merge these two renter's dilemmas. As we endeavour to remove clutter from our lives, we will also be freeing up valuable planting real estate. Furthermore, wicking beds can be expensive and difficult to set up on a larger scale, so this small space option eliminates a lot of the troubles, but still provides plenty of space for perennial herbs or big seasonal plants like tomatoes or pumpkin.

As the name suggests, a wicking bed is a self-watering garden bed. Like the wick in a prospector's oil lantern, the garden bed uses capillary attraction to draw water from a reservoir at the base of the bed. The reservoir can be refilled from a pipe at the top and plants will use the water as they require it, which is far more efficient than surface watering. The beauty of this wicking bed design is that it is also small enough to move, so unworthy stewards may be a thing of the past. Oh, and if you start accumulating stuff again, you can always turf out your plants and refill the bins with those old Chumbawumba albums.

1

Go into your shed (or wherever clutter gathers) and find an unbroken storage container.

Measure and cut the PVC pipe so that it extends from the base of the container to about 50 mm (2 in) taller than the rim. This is the **UPRIGHT WATER CHANNEL** through which the wicking bed will be filled.

2 >

3

Cut the PVC using a handsaw.

4

DRILL HOLES
all the way round the
water channel, with
most of the holes
concentrated towards
the bottom.

5

Affix the elbow
at the base of
the upright.

6

Measure about 250 mm (10 in) from
the top and mark a spot at the
centre of the container.

7

Use a 28 mm (1 in) drill bit to drill a large hole in the side of the bin. This will be the wicking bed's overflow valve.

Apply a bead of silicone glue to a 25 mm (1 in) PVC valve fitting. Press the valve into place, being **EXTRA CAREFUL** not to crack the bin. Silicone can take up to an hour to set, so this is a good opportunity to prepare yourself a snack.

8 »

‹ 9

Place the water channel assembly into the container, with the elbow at the bottom and the cap and upright channel at the top. Place the assembly in the corner – this will make filling the bin much easier.

< 10

Fill the container with expanded clay or scoria to just below the bottom edge of the overflow valve. Be careful when adding the scoria that you **DON'T CRACK** or damage the bin. One little leak will render the wicking bed useless.

Cut the Geotech fabric to fit **SNUGLY** over the top of the expanded clay. This will provide a permeable layer for water to move through, but prevent the soil level from dropping.

11 >

12

Make sure that the Geotech fabric also covers the overflow valve so that no soil escapes from the container.

‹ 13

Fill the remaining depth of the bin with a premium organic potting mix. Treat yourself to **THE GOOD STUFF** - the stuff that smells like Egyptian leather.

14

Call up your **BEST MATE** and invite them to help with a plant-out.

‹ 15

Fill the water channel until the overflow valve starts to drain. From now on, watering your plants will only require the occasional top-up every few days so you can focus your efforts on other things, like saving money to buy your own house.

PROJECT DETAILS

TIME 🕐

DIFFICULTY RATING ⛏️

BUDGET 🪙🪙

THINGS YOU'LL NEED...

- 2 windows
- paint scraper
- sandpaper
- wood putty
- paintbrush
- varnish or outdoor paint
- drill set or screwdriver
- set of door hinges
- 8 x 25 mm (1 in) timber screws
- 2 x 300 mm (12 in) lengths of light-duty chain (optional)
- 2 x 10 mm (½ in) screws

WINDOW FRAME GREENHOUSE

HOARDING NEVER LOOKED SO GOOD

Some materials are simply too valuable to throw away. In the case of my father, who is a loveable but well-established hoarder, all materials fall into that category. I spent countless summers pulling bits of wood or rusted metal out of a shed while he made a case for why each rotten weatherboard or rusted doorknob would come in handy later. It is worth mentioning that the very shed in question was assembled from such salvaged items. While there were certainly no right angles in this structure and it seemed to be held together by sheer willpower, it still remains standing today. I think my dad believed that when his building materials reached a critical point, they would spontaneously spawn yet another shanty.

While I mercifully did not inherit my dad's hoarding habit, we do share an affinity towards the collection of old window frames. As building standards continue to improve, vintage single pane windows are falling out of favour and seem to be finding their way to the curb or into skips. Being a gardener is about resourcefulness. Rather than see that history lost, we can upcycle windows into a simple, freestanding mini-greenhouse.

The mini-greenhouse is a great small space option for propagating seedlings and avoiding early-season frost damage. It is amazing how much heat can be trapped inside this simple structure, so don't overdo it once the weather starts to warm up. Our design enables you to collapse the structure so that it can be neatly stored away for the next season when it is no longer needed. Like all salvaged projects, a discerning eye and a little bit of elbow grease will go a long way to not only making this a functional part of the garden but, more importantly, making it an aesthetic feature that you can be proud of.

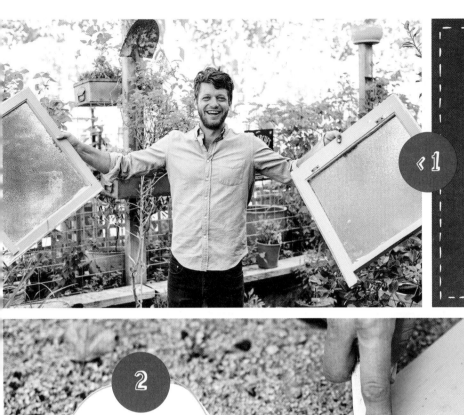

‹1

SALVAGE a set of old windows, ideally a matching set, but at least of similar size. Hardwood timber and something with minimal rot will make things easier, but it's not essential.

2

Use the paint scraper to knock away rough patches of paint on the frame and remove any large splinters.

‹3

Sand back the remaining paint until the frame is even and smooth. This process may reveal some **SURPRISING COLOURFUL LAYERS** underneath. It's all part of the history, baby.

Once the frame is cleaned up, fill in any imperfections with wood putty, which will stop water from infiltrating through weak parts of the wood and will greatly extend the lifetime of the frame.

A coat of clear varnish will help protect the frame and also seal in the **RUSTIC**, stripped-back look of the wood. Otherwise, lay on a few coats of your favourite paint.

< 4

5 >

< 6

Lay the window frames end to end on a flat surface and attach the door hinges. To avoid splitting the wood, pre-drill the holes before screwing the hinges on.

‹7 The frames should now be able to form a pitched greenhouse structure by closing the angle of the hinge and moving the windows upright. Expand the frames to your maximum desired size.

Set the maximum opening size by securing the two lengths of chain to either side of the greenhouse. Slide them down to the point in which each chain is **COMPLETELY TAUT** and fix them in place with a couple of 10 mm (½ in) screws. **8›**

Finally, a **VIEW** with a **ROOM!**

TOP 5

RECYCLED RAISED GARDEN BEDS

The raised garden bed is the holy grail of gardening infrastructure, because of the suite of qualities it brings to the patch. It allows you to import quality soil, chases the sunlight, is more ergonomic than a ground-level garden, drains well and, most importantly, looks shit hot. Here is a list of the hottest recycled or upcycled raised garden beds we know.

1
SINK

A sink is an obvious choice because it's easy to find and already equipped with great drainage. Many sinks are quite shallow by gardening standards, which makes them a prime vessel for salads and herbs. So much variety exists that almost anyone can find a sink that meets their aesthetic, so don't just pick any old thing off the street. Your Spidey senses should start tingling around the time of hard rubbish collection.

Where do trailers go when they die? The answer is to gardening heaven. If you are lucky enough to come across one of these, a trailer will provide an enormous growing area. We've had great success growing strawberries, and trailers have also proved ideal for growing crops that are hard to keep track of, such as potatoes. When it comes to harvest time you can simply empty the entire trailer out and know that you haven't missed any of the crop.

2
TRAILER

3

There is nothing cooler (see what we did there?) than those old-school aluminium-clad eskies from back in the day. You can still come across quite a few in country towns. If you can't locate one, try cladding a modern esky with a little corrugated tin. As we well know, drainage is no issue because there is already a ready-to-use spout built in. Another advantage is insulation, which will keep plants healthy by helping to normalise the soil temperature on those hot summer days, and in the cold winter months as well. Next time someone asks you to pass them a freshie, reach into the esky and pull out the good stuff.

There is nothing quite like those great cast-iron claw-footed beauties. As they become less and less common with the passage of time, the bathtub has become the white whale of the recycled raised garden bed world. The effort of transporting one of these is basically an activity in itself, and one not to be taken lightly. They are deep enough for virtually any crop, with room to let your plants sprawl. Try planting nasturtiums and strawberries around the edge, which will cascade over the side, thus imitating the flow of water. Is this art imitating nature or nature imitating life? We're not qualified to say, but whatever it is, we like it.

4

BATHTUB

5

WHEEL-BARROW

When retiring the old battleaxe of the working world, it is only fitting that it carry one final load. A wheelbarrow makes a perfect raised garden bed, ensuring there are many more years of companionship ahead of you. Make sure there is plenty of drainage and don't be afraid to take the drill to the old boy. Otherwise, the garden bed will slowly turn into a rotting bog. Once you are past that hurdle, the beauty, of course, is in its practicality and portability. Running late for a dinner party and have nothing to bring? How about a wheelbarrow full of farm-fresh herbs! Mum's getting on your case for not having a partner? Prove what a catch you are by introducing her to your wheelbarrow. Having trouble connecting with strangers and you can't understand why?

PROJECT LIST

So you think you've got what it takes to be the next hot gardener? Let's see what you're talking about. You think your compost doesn't stink? Sure, you've got some moves. I've seen you trellising those tomatoes, hanging that fruit high on the vine. People have been talking about the size of those pumpkins, too, but that doesn't impress me much. X-factor gardening is about more than just doing things right, it's about doing something new.

The veggie world is growing faster than a radish on seaweed extract and that means there are a multitude of new ideas bobbing to the surface. It is beyond exciting for us to see a strong edible gardening culture taking shape, dare we say ... taking root. When we started the business in 2008, it was such a niche market. Now there are more and more people trying to do the same work, and that means we all have a chance to raise the bar together. X-factor is about pushing the boundaries of what you can grow and how you can grow it. It's about being unconventional.

We discovered our own x-factor by mistake, when we had an opportunity to grow hops in the Melbourne CBD. Until then, as many of you would know, we only had eyes for tomatoes. We were conventional gardeners content with some good beans and fresh herbs, and there is nothing wrong with that. Hops and the infrastructure to support them were an entrance into a world beyond the basics. It made us think of other things that could be scaled down or scaled up to meet a new gardening challenge. Suddenly we were doing it ourselves, and that made us more aware of what was happening elsewhere in the world.

This chapter is for the tinkerers and innovators of the patch, those people who are constantly looking for a better way to do things. Pop Up Patch has been amazing for us in this sense, because it is a tiny gardening community where ideas are quickly shared. Our members are constantly inventing new ways to grow more in their square-metre patches and, as a result, we've watched some of the most elaborate and creative trellising systems take shape. One member tried to harness the power of wind and vegetables to make a small-scale water pump.

Of course, it doesn't always works out. But with every failed idea, there is progress towards something a little better. That's why we want to share some of our favourite x-factor gardening concepts, because inevitably some of our readers will say, 'Oh, that's cool, but I could do it better.' No-one has all the answers, and only by sharing can we come up with the next best thing together.

TIME

DIFFICULTY RATING

BUDGET

THINGS YOU'LL NEED...

- Togetherfarm blocks
- some form of imagination
- 50 x 75 mm (3 in) screws
- drill set
- 4 mm irrigation tubing (if irrigating by automatic timer)
- premium potting mix
- seedlings

X-FACTOR

GARDENING WITH BUILDING BLOCKS

WHEN BIG KIDS CAN FINALLY PLAY AGAIN

Lego can be credited for developing the creative minds of our modern-day engineers, so what better way to develop the minds of landscapers than by using Togetherfarm building blocks to build your own garden bed? This is a throwback to our younger years – when anything was possible – and other than your old, conservative mind there's no limit to your creation.

Finding the adventure in growing food is exactly what edible gardening is for us, and activities like this not only revitalise our relationship with the patch but help pull in those still sitting outside the veggie patch circle. More than that, they continue to change the perception that people who grow food need to have a beard and jump in excitement at the sight of good mulch.

This is yet another one of those classic DIY projects that I would have adored as a kid, but I simply didn't have the resources. But now, as an adult, I can indulge. If your loved ones let you, there will be no stopping how far you take this, and all ex-Lego builders will be getting that nervous twitch that strikes just before they *have* to build something big.

Togetherfarm blocks are made from 100% recycled and recyclable, UV-protected plastic. This is not a sales pitch – there's just no hiding that this is a quality, ethically made product. Before you plan some extended leave to conquer this activity, we should warn you that these blocks can only be purchased from the USA. There is some cost, and length of time, you will need to endure to get your hands on the bricks and mortar, so plan your life accordingly.

Like a pig in ... Mat with his building blocks and inner child about to be released! If working on a hard surface, it's a good idea to have some **DRAINAGE** underneath for the water to escape. Otherwise, you will have to deal with some water overflow. Really, it's not a huge deal, just worth mentioning.

< 1

2

Start creating ... Do we really need to explain how to use Lego?!

One nice design feature of these blocks is that they have screw threads that allow you to secure your creation so that bigger kids can't come over and thieve or knock it over. So, as you **CONSTRUCT** each level, pop in a screw to hold it together. It also keeps things sturdy, and that helps in the building process.

< 3

》》

Rather than having irrigation lines buried in underneath and through the soil, or placed over the top of the blocks, there is a hole that runs through each join that allows 4 mm poly tubing to fit through. It is best to run this tubing through as you build, rather than at the end.

< 4

When time, money and the killjoys say enough is enough, it's almost tools down and the necessary moment to **ADMIRE YOUR WORK**. Bring in the family – keeping the little kids away – and behold the wonder!

5 >

6

Now, fill with premium potting mix, ready for planting.

Plant a selection of seasonal vegetables and herbs. With your building block garden so **WONDROUS AND COLOURFUL**, even weeds would look great in this. We, however, prefer varieties that are more palatable.

< 7

Ignore what the other kids say. Your creation is not only wondrous, but productively wondrous. They're just jealous!

PATCH FAVOURITE

PROJECT DETAILS

TIME 🕐 🕐

DIFFICULTY RATING

BUDGET 💰 💰

THINGS YOU'LL NEED...

- newspaper or tarp
- 3 x 4 m (13 ft 1½ in) lengths of 20 mm (¾ in) electrical conduit
- spray paint
- crate
- 12 x 25 mm (1 in) U-brackets
- drill set
- 40 x 25 mm (1 in) timber screws
- bird netting
- 1.83 m x 2.5 m (6 ft x 8 ft 2½ in) sheet of heavy-duty clear plastic
- household stapler and staples
- 2 x 1.2 m (3 ft 11 in) medium wooden dowels
- staple gun and staples
- twine or string
- 1.83 m x 2.5 m (6 ft x 8 ft 2½ in) piece of shade cloth

VERSATILE HOOP HOUSE

THE SWISS ARMY KNIFE OF VEGETABLE GARDENING

The idea of transformation has always captivated me and I don't think I'm the only one. We all love the idea of something that is not what it seems. Or, I should say, something that is more than it appears to be. Transformers were 'more than meets the eye'. Superheroes all have secret identities because, presumably, the world can't handle their true nature other than in bite-sized doses. James Bond, though, is the ultimate – a normal guy with a staggering array of cool gadgets. Kind of like my childhood friend Kenny who had a watch that doubled as a calculator. Mathematics never seemed so cool.

While the Little Veggie Patch Co research and development department runs on a slightly tighter budget than MI6 or Wayne Enterprises, we have repurposed more than our share of unassuming materials. Salvaging and upcycling is all about unlocking the potential in a discarded item. Take the apple crate, for example. It started as a storage bin, yet we have used them as raised garden beds, chook coops, sand boxes and cubby houses. Trench mesh bars, typically used in concrete work, have become our staple trellising material. So imagine our excitement when we discovered electrical conduit.

Electrical conduit is a sturdy yet flexible poly tube used to house wiring. We discovered its usefulness while trying to sort out the problem of crappy pre-made net structures for our crates. Everything we had found before was confusing and impractical. Products inevitably had too many separate parts and would turn to twisted tangles of PVC and netting under even the slightest hint of wind. Thus, the conduit hoop house was born. Like the best things in the garden, it is simple, sturdy and inexpensive. Like a gadget fit for Bond, this easy hoop structure can transform into a greenhouse using bird netting or shade cloth.

1

Lay out a tarp or some newspaper on the ground. This will be the **FOUNDATION** of your paint workshop.

Electrical conduit comes in a generic PVC grey that speaks more to a building site than a peaceful garden, so lay the conduit out on the newspaper or tarp and spray paint it with two coats of your favourite colour.

2 ›

‹ 3

While the paint is drying, prepare the crate by attaching three sets of U-brackets on opposite sides of the crate.
Fix these at each end and through the centre. Fix a corresponding row below.

»

4

Two U-brackets above and below will keep the conduit from wiggling from side to side.

5

Slide the conduit into the U-brackets and bend over the top to the opposite side.

6

BEND the conduit in-line to create an extended HOOP STRUCTURE like an old-school poly tunnel.

‹ 7

Screw in a few 25 mm (1 in) timber screws along the edge of the crate. These will be used to hold your netting in place.

8

Throw bird netting over the top to get a sense of how it fits.

››

< 9

Stretch the netting at the bottom and **PULL IT TAUT**. The screws will do a good job holding it in place and will ensure it's not too fiddly or time-consuming.

Now it's time to build a **GREENHOUSE**. Cut thick construction plastic into a long strip – 1.2 m by 2 m (3 ft 11 in by 6 ft 6½ in). The width should match that of your crate and the strip should be long enough to reach the other side.

10 >

11

Fold the plastic over on itself, making a loop on one edge. Apply a liberal amount of staples, using a household stapler.

Feed a wooden dowel through the loop of plastic that you just made. This will provide **A LITTLE WEIGHT** for your greenhouse attachment and prevent the plastic from blowing off.

< **12**

13

Use a staple gun to attach the non-dowel edge of the plastic midway up the side of the crate.

The greenhouse is now ready for action. Unroll it and spread the plastic over the top. Notice how the wooden dowel **ANCHORS** the system.

< **14**

>>

15

When not in use, the plastic can be rolled up on itself and tied to the side with twine or string.

‹ 16

The shade cloth is built exactly the same as our plastic cover. Cut to the appropriate dimensions and attach a 1.2 m (3 ft 11 in) wooden dowel or timber length to one end. Use a staple gun to fix the non-dowel end of the cloth to the opposite side of the crate to the plastic. It can now be extended or stored away according to your needs.

Here it is! Give yourself a pat on the back. This is the holy grail of patch **VERSATILITY** – cool in the summer and warm in the winter.

PROJECT DETAILS

TIME

DIFFICULTY RATING

BUDGET

THINGS YOU'LL NEED...

- courage
- glazed pot
- masking tape
- spray paints, including undercoat
- retro wire pot stand

A FASHIONABLE POT
MUTTON DRESSED AS LAMB

- - - ⌾ - - -

We're not afraid to follow or reject a trend, and over the years we've fallen for both the good and bad that fashion has had to offer. Hindsight is a wonderful thing in so many parts of life, but particularly when it comes to decisions about styling.

In our minds it seems to be taking about 20 years to overcome the embarrassment of decisions once made. The 00s revitalised the 80s and now the 10s are doing the same for the 90s. Thankfully so. I've been waiting more than two decades to justify the undercut I had when I was 14, and finally I get my chance. A few more years and I will dust off my rollerblades.

Of course, we should not only be living for the chance to recycle old fashions and outlive embarrassment. There are still people, out there on the edge, exposing themselves to the mocking and the taunting and the potential humiliation that can come from making courageous decisions. And these are the visionaries confronting us with fashions we can choose to either reject or follow.

While some may think gardening and fashion are worlds apart, in fact they run in parallel. In our minds, the key to edible gardening – all gardening for that matter – is about looking and feeling good about what you are doing. Only then do you keep coming back for more.

So, don't worry about what all the naysayers and the Johnny-come-latelys have to say: a painted, colourful pot will stand the test of time. It will stand the test of time or we will happily wait 20 years to prove it.

Play stylist here and determine what colours will work together well. This is not the same as throwing on a few clothes from the wardrobe and discovering to your shock that it looks good. This is permanent paint, and a pot, that your friends will see every time they come over. We're talking a **STATEMENT** here.

‹1

2

Choose your pattern and start taping. We favour a solid band with a random zig-zag. Like, whatever.

The worst thing you can do is cramp your design. Let it breathe or it will quickly turn stale. The **FASHION** demands sharp lines so ensure you tape with intent.

‹3

4

Review your work in progress and cover all areas that risk catching a stray spray of colour.

5

Spraying on an undercoat is a shrewd step. It gives the real star of the show the best foundation to perform.

Allow the undercoat to dry for 15–20 minutes before applying the colour. Once again, allow that to dry for 15–20 minutes and give an all-important second coating.

6 >

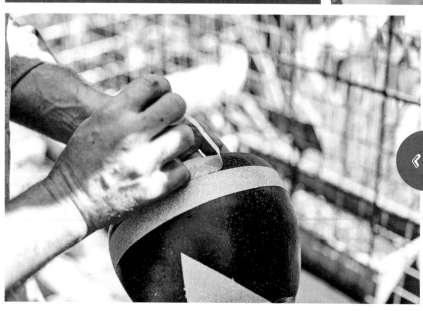

< 7

Once the paint has dried, begin to reveal your **MASTERPIECE** by carefully peeling off the tape.

Find it pride of place on an **UBER-COOL WIRE STAND**, perhaps in a light-filled entrance somewhere, so that it can house an edible plant. Herbs will be the most hardy and tolerant plants to use.

< 8

This **FABULOUS** pot is more than simple fashion, darling. It is super practical, as this is where we pick our garnish herbs, yaah.

PROJECT DETAILS

TIME

DIFFICULTY RATING

BUDGET

THINGS YOU'LL NEED...

- hops rhizomes
- recycled apple crate
- food-safe black plastic (builders film)
- staple gun and staples
- carpenter's square and marker
- jigsaw or circular saw
- 1 cypress pine post: 3.6 m x 100 mm/100 mm (11 ft 9½ in x 4 in/4 in)
- void former or old plastic pots and styrofoam boxes
- weed mat
- 1 cypress pine length: 3.6 m x 90 mm/45 mm (11 ft 9½ in x 3½ in/1¾ in)
- 10 x 70 mm (2¾ in) bulge head screws
- drill set
- 8 eyelets
- 2 x 10 m (32 ft 9½ in) ropes
- spirit level
- 10 x 30-litre (27-quart) bags of premium potting mix
- 50 m (164 ft) coarse twine
- ladder

HOPS TOWER

LET THEM GROW HOPS AND DRINK BEER, PLEASE

Over the years we have extended our growing repertoires and explored varieties that don't necessarily end up on the kitchen stove. And that's not just the inedibles that turned out too foul to digest, but ingredients that go into making other stuff, like beer. So when Little Creatures Brewery asked us to grow them some hops it was not only a push into new territory, but also a crowning moment for the business that completed us.

There is a glitch in the human condition that when someone asks you to do something and puts the word 'beer' alongside or in the vicinity of it, 'yes' will generally follow. So, as soon as we were asked to grow the hops, we had already committed to it without giving it so much as a glimmer of thought. Then we needed to work out how it grew.

As we have since worked out, hops is unlike anything we've grown before. Hops is the ultimate vertical grower. It exclusively grows skywards. Not horizontally, not down to the ground, but vertically, as in up, and up, and up and up. As soon as you give it a non-vertical path to follow, it will just begin flailing about. It will then stall growing, waiting for you to fix the situation – and if you don't, it will wilt and brown off.

It is the first time we have come across a plant that seems to have a fear of ground level – but hops is that plant, with this unique fear. So, to grow it, you need something akin to a tower to satisfy this requirement.

At their peak, hops vines shoot up to 30 cm (12 in) per day. That's pretty impressive and will give you an idea of the scale of the tower required, but listen – have you ever heard a plant grow? The growing pains of the vine are so immense, it is suggested that you can actually hear them.

< 1

Source some hops rhizomes. These are root structures from which the vines will sprout. Hops are dormant in winter, and anyone wanting to grow hops will need some dormant root structures to make a start. Approaching spring is the best time to source them. Look online – there will be a few people and places selling a number of varieties with names such as **FUGGLES**, **KENT GOLDINGS** and **CASCADE**.

2

Line the sides of your recycled apple crate with some food-safe black plastic.

< 3

Measure a 100 mm (4 in) square in the absolute centre of the crate into which the 100 mm (4 in) cypress pine post will slot and anchor itself.

4

Using a jigsaw or a circular saw with a bit of finesse, cut out the centred 100 mm (4 in) square.

Because the crate will hold a bit of soil, it's best to build a false bottom that will stop the pressure build-up. A simple solution is to purchase or recycle a void former – a styrofoam pod used in the building industry. One that is 150–300 mm (6–12 in) in depth will suit. Push it into the base of the crate. It will be a very **SNUG FIT** (nice!).

5 ›

‹ 6

If you don't have a void former, you can use plastic pots as an alternative. Simply build a false bottom using old plastic pots, covered over with styrofoam boxes for extra strength. This will elevate the soil height. First, build your pots up. Once you are satisfied with the level of the pots, place styrofoam boxes upside down over the top, which will create a relatively even, flat base.

‹ 7

Cut out a 100 mm (4 in) square in the centre of the pod (or styrofoam) to reveal the slot hole.

8

Place weed mat over the top to ensure the soil does not fall through, but make sure there is passage for the water to drain freely.

‹ 9

Once again, leave the hole in the centre clear. We know there's a lot of fuss over this one hole, but it will soon be worth it.

Measure and cut your 90 mm/45 mm (3½ in/1¾ in) piece of timber into three even 1.2 m (3 ft 11 in) lengths. Two of these lengths will be used to form the cross.

‹ 10

Using a 70 mm (2¾ in) bulge head screw, attach one 1.2 m (3 ft 11 in) length of timber to the end of the 100 mm (4 in) cypress pine post. Make sure it's centred as we're forming the first phase of the cross for the hops to climb.

11 ›

12

Now, attach the second 1.2 m (3 ft 11 in) length on top of the first to complete the cross.

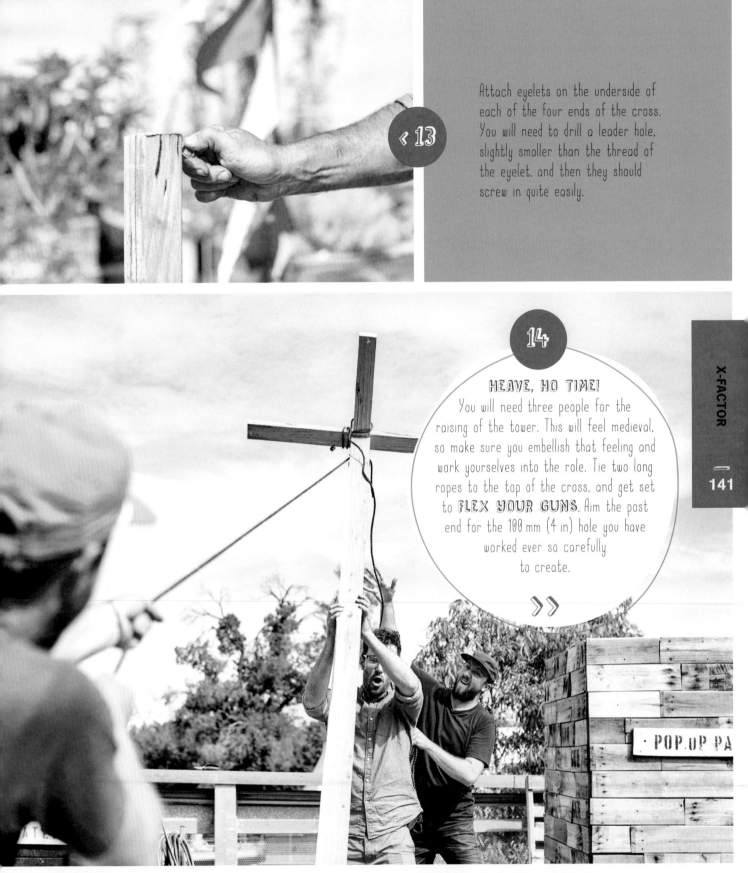

‹ 13

Attach eyelets on the underside of each of the four ends of the cross. You will need to drill a leader hole, slightly smaller than the thread of the eyelet, and then they should screw in quite easily.

14

HEAVE, HO TIME!

You will need three people for the raising of the tower. This will feel medieval, so make sure you embellish that feeling and work yourselves into the role. Tie two long ropes to the top of the cross, and get set to **FLEX YOUR GUNS**. Aim the post end for the 100 mm (4 in) hole you have worked ever so carefully to create.

»

‹ 15

Once the post has slotted through all the way to the bottom – you should feel it clunk down to ground level – have your help hold the tower upright, checking with the spirit level that it's perfectly vertical. As it stands it's a death trap of biblical proportions, so it will need to be braced.

Use the last 1.2 m (3 ft 11 in) length of 90 mm/45 mm (3½ in/1¾ in) cypress for your brace. It should fit quite snugly inside the apple crate but will need **REINFORCING**. First, screw it to each side of the crate, using a 70 mm (2¾ in) bulge head screw on either side.

16 ›

17

Now that the brace is secured to the crate, it's time to secure the post to the brace. Add two 70 mm (2¾ in) bulge head screws to make sure it's secured. We're now helping out each other.

18

Fill up the crate with a premium potting mix.

«19

Screw four eyelets on each side of the cypress pine post at soil level, and in the middle of the top panels of the crate.

20 Now, thread the coarse twine from one of the eyelets at the bottom of the post to the top, and back down to the opposing one on the crate. Cut and tie off securely. You'll need a **STEADY LADDER** for this step.

21 Repeat this on all four sides. Now the climbing course is set for the vine. Rather than trying to unwind the vine or pull the hops using a ladder at harvest time, growers will cut the twine down and **HARVESTING** will take place at the safer ground level.

22

Plant the hop vine in the crate, burying it under enough soil to cover all its roots and shoots. Position the shoots – from which the vine will grow – so they are pointing skywards. As soon as the weather heats up, the rhizomes will come alive and the vine will start its climb. The vine begins its **GROWTH** in mid-spring and is harvested by late summer or early autumn.

SEEDLINGS

PROJECT DETAILS

TIME

DIFFICULTY RATING

BUDGET

THINGS YOU'LL NEED...

- some pretty handy skills
- 4 x 1.8 m (5 ft 11 in) hardwood stakes
- measuring tape
- carpenter's square
- marker
- 12 x L-brackets
- drill set
- 12 x 20 mm (¾ in) timber screws
- spirit level
- 8 x 40 mm (1½ in) timber screws
- 1 x 6 m x 2.4 m (19 ft 8 in x 7 ft 10½ in) sheet of reo mesh (with plenty of leftovers)
- bolt cutters or angle grinder
- cable ties

THE ULTIMATE TOMATO TRELLIS

TOMATO CITY

Serious tomato growers are serious people – particularly when it comes to growing tomatoes – and there is a hidden culture built around these people and the trellising systems they use. Being part of a sub-culture is all about walking a fine line. You need to strike the balance between recognition of invention and ingenuity, along with managing the secrecy and legend of the group.

As tomato culture emerges into a popular one, the trellising systems that people use to grow their plants are beginning to receive more attention and the race is now on to design and build the definitive system. We don't see this move into the mainstream as a threat, but instead an opportunity to harvest bigger and better ideas for the greater good. And we have some of our own.

An ultimate tomato trellis, for a serious grower, cannot be a single unit designed for a single plant. No-one entrenched in the tomato culture grows only a single tomato when in season, so the ultimate trellis needs to accommodate many plants. The system also needs to be sturdy so that it will endure years of good service. The ultimate system should be a loyal one.

We have always enjoyed playing around with stakes and twine, but this is a little more serious. There will be lots of foliage and lots of fruit relying on this system, so your hands need to be splinter-free. For that reason, we're calling in the big guns! It's a material that every Italian tomato grower has a great affinity for: concrete reinforcing mesh!

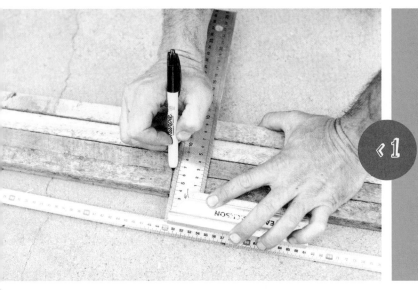

‹1

In actual fact, I lied about the **SPLINTER** part. There are four long wooden stakes in this set-up and therefore plenty of potential to gather some splinters. These stakes will provide the braces to hold the trellis frames. To each stake, you'll need to attach three L-brackets, so measure down 600 mm (1 ft 11½ in) and 1.2 m (3 ft 11 in) from the top of the stakes..

Attach each L-bracket using a 20 mm (¾ in) screw. One will be right at the top and then one at 600 mm (1 ft 11½ in) and the final one at 1.2 m (3 ft 11 in).

2›

3

Repeat for all four stakes and then go grab the tweezers to get to work on Round 1 of your splinters.

››

‹4 It's time to attach the four wooden stakes to each corner of the crates. Have the L-brackets facing out and use a spirit level to make sure they are perfectly level.

When securing the stakes to the crate, make sure they are all set at the same level. We drive each stake 300 mm (12 in) underground and then use two 40 mm (1½ in) timber screws to fix them to the crate.

5›

‹6 With the stakes in and secured properly, that's the FRAMEWORK installed. It's finally time to get into some power tools!

‹ 7

It's time to prepare the reo mesh. Cut three 1.2 m (3 ft 11 in) squares using either hefty bolt cutters or an angle grinder – each small square in the reo grid is 200 mm (8 in), so count out six of these smaller squares to get the right length for the large squares.

Taking three of the squares you have cut, two will need to be altered. Take one and cut out the internal bars to leave (effectively) a window frame and cross through its centre (four squares).

8 ›

‹ 9

With the next square, there is a little less to cut out. This time, discard enough to leave you with a 3 x 3 of nine squares. The final large square does not require cutting.

››

BOTTOM

These three frames
will be used to create the
levels of the **ULTIMATE**
tomato trellis, the most
open one at the lowest
point and the untouched
mesh at the
highest point.

MIDDLE

TOP

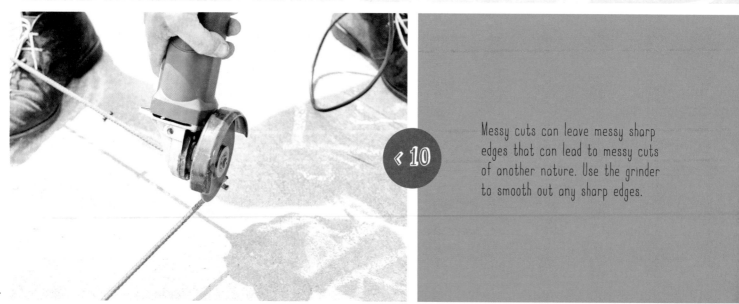

< 10

Messy cuts can leave messy sharp
edges that can lead to messy cuts
of another nature. Use the grinder
to smooth out any sharp edges.

Start by slipping the bottom window frame segment over the top of the stakes and then slide it down to the bottom level of brackets.

< 12

To **SECURE** the mesh properly we could get a welder and show off our craft, but we want to be able to dismantle this easily and put it aside when the season is over, so a small cable tie will work well. Cable tie each corner to each bracket.

>>

13

Now, slide on the second level. This is the 3 x 3 grid and holds the majority of the tomatoes.

Finally, the third frame and top level of this trellising system is about to be unleashed on some new spring tommies.

14 ›

‹ 15

Plant the new season tomatoes. This system accommodates four **BEAUTIES**, so centre them under your lower level grid. for their initial climb, they'll need a small stake for support. but once they reach the trellis, they'll be supported beautifully.

A serious system for some **SERIOUS TOMATOES**

TOP 5

X-FACTOR CREATIONS AT OUR FAVOURITE JOB

By now you're off your Veggie Patch training wheels and are looking to play with the big kids. This edible gardening thing is contagious and we don't blame you for wanting to lift your game. Here's a look at one of our favourite projects – The Little Creatures Brewery in Geelong – and our top five pieces that helped us graduate to the next level.

1 CONCRETE MIXER OLIVE PLANTER

This piece sits at the entrance point to the hospitality area, and is a nice reveal just as you walk around the corner. No doubt my dad's work in the concrete industry had a huge influence over this one, and he hooked us up with an old concrete mixer, sourced from an industrial graveyard. We had its top cracked open like an egg and the old paint sand-blasted to reveal a new coating of metal that would quickly rust. A base plate was attached to avoid any potential catastrophes. The greatest challenge was planting it out, and the mixer holds a mature olive tree. This tree is sister to an olive tree that lives at the original Little Creatures brewery in Fremantle. We like that connection for the business – and the fact that I grew up there too, where my dad had a job at Cockburn (understandably pronounced 'Coburn') Cement.

Just down the road from the brewery, we found a sweet trash and treasure store that had a mountain of old rusty sultana boxes. A bit of negotiation and we secured 50 of them at what we thought was a steal – until a few weeks later when we got 50 more for half that price. The baskets are purpose-built for a hanging wall garden. There are little holes all over the boxes that provide perfect drainage and ample hooking opportunities to secure them to a wall. Attaching them to the highest point on this wall was a test of both our nerve and our cherry picker driving skills, but raising the bar never comes easy.

2 SULTANA BASKET WALL GARDEN

3
WROUGHT IRON PLANTING PIPES

Maybe it's our affinity with all things rusty, or maybe it's because we like a physical challenge, but getting these pipes to stand tall nearly gave us hernias. These pipes are made from old-school wrought iron, and the weight is staggering. Really staggering. For that reason, rolling them into the zone was immensely satisfying, but standing them tall was immensely challenging. Once standing tall, they are the ultimate death trap. So, rather than playing wrought-iron roulette with the beer-drinking patrons, we welded metal tabs on the bases and bolted them into the ground.

We also had the privilege of exploring the old treasure left lying around the site, which comprised a couple of hundred years of history – real quality junk. There is nothing better than junk diving, free of charge. Perhaps the most satisfying part of this was comparing what we found to prices at the trash and treasure store, and we spent much time distracted by the potential side business this could create. Amongst the treasure were these old wind turbines, which made nice little wall planters when bolted to the 19th-century brick walls.

4
WIND TURBINE

5
DRINKING TROUGH FLOWERBED

Finally, a piece that isn't old and rusty – rather a slightly mis-manufactured drinking trough. Little Creatures asked if we could find any to use as drinking stations, and while searching we became distracted with the idea of using the faulty versions as neat little flowerbeds. Though they're made from durable stainless steel, the fact that someone, or something, messed up a bolt point or depth gauge means they will never meet spec for school drinking fountains. However, their imperfections make little difference when planting flowers or herbs in them. They come with all the bolts and brackets to mount them to a wall, so you save on the hardware, too.

PROJECT LIST

VERTICAL GARDENING

It's not how big it is, but how you use it. That's certainly true of vertical gardening. As big, spacious blocks of land fall by the wayside, we need to find more creative ways of using what we have efficiently. Growing things up a wall, or hanging over a railing, or on top of your head if you wish, are ways of chasing the sun to grow food. In some cases, they are the only opportunities we have to start a veggie patch.

The popularity of wall gardening has grown as our living spaces have compacted, and growing things vertically now occurs more through necessity than just gardening freestyle. Sure, we still like to wall garden because it looks good and helps fill up an otherwise vacant and stark slab of brick, concrete or timber – but it is quickly becoming the most practical way to grow edibles for many people.

When we hold our edible gardening workshops, the first thing we talk about is aspect – that is, what direction to face your veggie patch. If you have read some gardening literature you will know that it's best to face the patch north in the southern hemisphere and south in the northern hemisphere, but what if a three-storey building stands in between you and the sunshine? What if that building is even bigger?

Old gardening principles have needed to evolve as our cities have grown up, and we've had to grow up a little too, positioning our veggie patches high on walls to chase the sun. Aspect is irrelevant when your house sits in the middle of a major city. It is all about going up and getting creative about the options at hand.

To know whether the wall will be suitable for growing food is an easy reconnaissance mission. Get out a garden chair, put on a pot of coffee and track the flow of sunlight on the prospective wall. If the wall gets sun in winter, it will more than likely get sun – and more of it – in summer. A little knowledge about load bearings and some handiness are also useful when weighing up how you propose to grow food vertically.

Rather than Googling 'load bearings of a wall', get advice from someone who is professionally trained and takes these things more seriously than you. While the motivation of growing food runs strong – Daniel-son – safety should be paramount.

In this chapter, we map out five simple DIYs, so you'll be spoiled for choice when it comes to deciding how to make your wall productive and use your space more wisely.

PROJECT DETAILS

TIME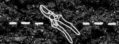

DIFFICULTY RATING

BUDGET

THINGS YOU'LL NEED...

- measuring tape
- pencil or marker
- 1 x cypress pine length:
  2.4 m x 70 mm/19 mm
  (7 ft 10½ in x 2¾ in/¾ in)
- handsaw
- spirit level
- 4 x 50 mm (2 in) bulge head
  screws
- drill set
- wall garden modules
- 12 x 25 mm (1 in) timber screws
- premium potting mix
- seedlings
- water

Note: When selecting plants, remember that those with shallow root systems do best in these small, confined spaces.

MODULAR VERTICAL GARDENING
DON'T GROW UP TOO FAST

As we have always said, any wall that basks in the glory of sunshine is a wall waiting to have things grown on it. Whether it is timber, brick, concrete or even metal, the wall in question can most certainly be adapted to growing. A green wall is a far better alternative to an empty one, giving you meaningful and productive real estate in the most unlikely of places. What's more, if you live in an urban environment, this may very well be your only available option.

In recent years, the proliferation of modular systems has made wall gardening more accessible to all. Even the most moderately handy people – and I include myself in this category – can create what appear to be grand feats of engineering. Just because it's easier doesn't make it bad. In fact, it is quite the opposite. Anything that gets more people outside and growing something should be celebrated. Modular systems not only empower people to dictate the size of their wall garden by using small units that link together, it also allows for seamless expansion when desired.

Bearing in mind that the wall garden can always be extended further, take it slowly and see how your relationship develops. Start with a few modules and slowly add more commitment and responsibility as you adjust to wall garden life. The worst thing to do is overcommit and suddenly find yourself in over your head, surrounded by plants you don't even recognise and trying to live up to their expectations. Even if you feel pressure from friends and family with large, long-term wall gardens, take it at your own pace. Steps forward are easier than steps backwards, so what's the rush?

SWEET BABY SPINACH! That's a great wall!

‹ 1

Choose a wall that receives 4-6 hours of direct or filtered light per day. North-facing walls are ideal, as they will gather extra sun in the winter, when light can often be hard to come by. Morning light is gentler than the afternoon, so an east-facing wall is also a good choice.

The size of your wall garden will, of course, correlate to the size of your appetite, but let the height be determined by what is manageable to harvest. **WATERING** and **HARVESTING** are easier on a human scale, so start with what you can reach. You can always upgrade to a ladder or cherry picker later. Measure the wall dimensions accordingly.

2 ›

‹ 3

We want our wall garden to cover roughly 1.2 m (3 ft 11¼ in) vertically and it will only have enough room for a single column of units. Cut two 1.2 m (3 ft 11¼ in) lengths of our cypress pine. These will act as wall mounts.

4

Measure the distance between mounting points on the modular unit. In our case, this distance is 450 mm (1 ft 5½ in).

Attach the top of the first timber using the appropriate hardware for the type of wall. For our standard timber fence, 50 mm (2 in) bulge head screws will be strong enough to hold the weight and are just the right length to not annoy the neighbours on the other side. If in doubt, ask a friendly attendant at the hardware store.

5 ›

‹ 6

Use a spirit level to make sure that the timber is plum before **COMMITTING** to the bottom screw.

< 7 Attach the second timber at 450 mm (1¾ in). This will ensure that the timbers slot neatly into the recess at the back of the wall garden module.

Use the spirit level to make sure that the second timber is **PERFECTLY VERTICAL**. With both panels now securely attached, use a spirit level to mark the placement for each wall garden unit. In our case, each module is 200 mm (8 in) in height and needs about 50 mm (2 in) of **BREATHING ROOM** between units, so we marked 250 mm (10 in) intervals.

8 >

< 9 Measure and affix the mounting screws on which the module will hang. Use 25 mm (1 in) timber screws, leaving about 5–10 mm (¼–½ in) protruding from the timber.

< 10 Before filling up the modules, make sure they attach without any hassles. You may have put the screws in, but it's worth **DOUBLE-CHECKING** that they're secure. Adjust anything that is out of place.

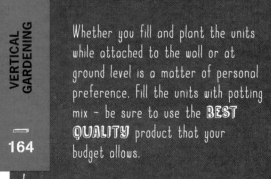

Whether you fill and plant the units while attached to the wall or at ground level is a matter of personal preference. Fill the units with potting mix – be sure to use the **BEST QUALITY** product that your budget allows.

11 >

12 Plant the seedlings and water them in.

< 13

You probably noticed that each unit has drainage holes at the bottom. **GOOD SLEUTHING!** You need only water the topmost unit and gravity will do the rest of the work for you.

Casually stand near your wall garden and let the cat calls start rolling in.

FOR RENT

PROJECT DETAILS

TIME

DIFFICULTY RATING

BUDGET

THINGS YOU'LL NEED...

- milk crate
- hessian coffee sack
- large double-sided hook
- scissors (if needed)
- a railing, the side of a crate, a hole in the wall, any suitable place to hang your planter
- 30-litre (27-quart) bag of premium organic potting mix
- favourite plant
- water

HANGING MILK CRATE PLANTER
THE STRONG FLAT WHITE OF THE PATCH

Vertical gardening is often challenging, but not always. There are occasions when a wall garden is little more than a milk crate, hessian bag and a hook, and so is the case with the hanging milk crate planter. Here is an example of one very popular culture providing just about everything you'll need. The culture in question is the coffee-drinking one, and living in Melbourne – a city that harbours an unhealthy obsession with it – means that the gear you'll need is on hand everywhere.

Any coffee drinker should be able to source the materials for this one. If you're not really interested in coffee, but are more than interested in this activity, make friends with some drinkers or at the very least start loitering outside busy cafes. There you should find a stray milk crate and, if you get your timing and approach right, a hessian sack.

After years of collecting discarded milk crates for this and many other purposes, we are still unsure whether this product is considered legal tender. Does someone own them – as is the case with pallets? Did they just forget to pick them up? Why do they treat them with such contempt?

As you're walking down the street with your milk crate, considering all these questions, all that is left is a trip to the hardware store to collect a big hook and a bag of good-quality potting mix. While it's beautiful just how simple this system is, one of the mysteries of the trash world remains unsolved.

You will find empty milk crates **DISCARDED** on every street corner and within every nook and loneway in the city. I'm not sure who started the complete disregard for this product, but it means that finding one is easy.

〈 1

The hessian coffee sack can be a little harder to acquire for it seems to hold **GREATER VALUE**. Anyone who's anyone needs to know a barista in the city, and thankfully we're anyone.

2 〉

First step of construction is lining the crate with the hessian sack. Because it will be too large for the crate, it will need to be folded back down, but the finish will be quite neat.

〈 3

Use the hook to break a hole in the sack from where it will hang. If you're having trouble piercing the sack, use scissors. The hook should go through the top part of the milk crate centrally, so that it **HANGS EVENLY** with the veggie patch.

< 4

Now, hook the crate over your railing. The hook we are using is large enough to hang it from a veggie crate, but the size of your hanging edge/railing will determine the size of the hook you use. Obviously you need to position the crate so that it receives good sunlight.

5 >

< 6

Fill up the hessian-lined milk crate with premium organic potting mix. One 30-litre (27-quart) bag is bang on the money.

PATCH FAVOURITE

TIME

DIFFICULTY RATING

BUDGET

THINGS YOU'LL NEED…

- a sturdy pallet in good condition
- handsaw or circular saw
- reciprocating saw
- measuring tape
- pencil
- spirit level
- drill set
- 25 x 50 mm (2 in) timber screws
- dust mask and safety equipment for ears and eyes
- sandpaper or electric sander
- 8 x 50 mm (2 in) bulge head screws
- 2 x L-brackets
- 1 m x 1 m (3 ft 3½ in x 3 ft 3½ in) piece of plastic lining
- staple gun and staples or pin nails and hammer
- premium organic potting mix
- ladder (if needed)
- variety of seedlings (dependent on season and sun exposure of chosen location)
- water

PALLET WALL GARDEN
A MORE REFINED PALLET

Over the past few years the pallet has slowly crept from the fringes of my awareness into a full-blown obsession. I dream of pallet houses and sleeping in a pallet bed. Perhaps even setting out over the horizon in my pallet boat. Such is the scope and scale of their flexibility that you're only limited by imagination and the ability to acquire enough pallets. This, of course, may be the sticking point – acquisition.

Pallets are owned by their maker and, in theory, will be reused. However, there does seem to be a large discrepancy between the theory and the practice. Let it be known that we advise against and do not condone any sort of theft. Yet a walk down a laneway will inevitably reveal more than a few seemingly abandoned pallets. Alas, this is where we enter a moral and ethical grey area. If in doubt, consult the business owner. If no such individual is available, one must consult the angel and devil on either shoulder. In my case, unfortunately, the devil will likely win out, being both more experienced and skilled at navigating the landscape of my mind.

Aligning with the prevalence of pallets is the increased emphasis on wall gardens. Recently, the market has been full of new modules, racks or hangers to make the most of that once unproductive space. Yet, the most pivotal moment for me was the realisation that the pallet is basically a ready-built wall garden in itself. There is no need to rush out and buy the latest and greatest technology when there is already an elegant solution leaning against that laneway wall. Two great things coming together? I haven't been this excited since Michael Jordan and Nike teamed up to make me jump higher.

The trick to any good salvage project is keeping it as true to its original form as possible, thus eliminating extra work. The pallet wall garden is no exception – it requires very little refitting and hardware to go vertical. Oh, and unlike those Air Jordans, this project will actually deliver what was promised.

Source a sturdy pallet in reasonable condition that you wouldn't mind seeing on your wall for the next fifty years. This is the beginning of a **WONDERFUL NEW FRIENDSHIP.**

< 1

Cut the pallet in half (just next to the central timber) using your trusty handsaw. This will really get the blood flowing and **BUILD EXCITEMENT** for the project.

2 >

Strip down the pallet offcut using a reciprocating saw to cut through the nails. The timber lengths will be used to bolster the other half of the pallet.

< 3

>>

‹4 ‹1 ‹2

While you have the reciprocating saw out, cut the middle two timbers from the pallet wall garden.

5 ›

Use 50 mm (2 in) timber screws to attach the lengths back on to the pallet. They should now be snug against the nearest timber. These will be your planting zones.

‹1 ‹2

6

Grab a scrap length from the section that you cut down and screw it to the front of the pallet. You will now have one planting section that is two boards deep front and back.

‹ 7

Screw another length of timber to the second planting zone. There should now be two distinct planting sections on the pallet, each side two boards deep.

8

Grab two timber lengths and drill a series of holes at 40 mm (1½ in) intervals. These will be drainage holes for the bottom planter box. Use a 10–15 mm (½ in) drill bit.

‹ 9

Attach a pre-drilled base timber to the bottom of the pallet. No cutting or fitting will be necessary. Secure the length with two 50 mm (2 in) timber screws at each end and the middle of the pallet.

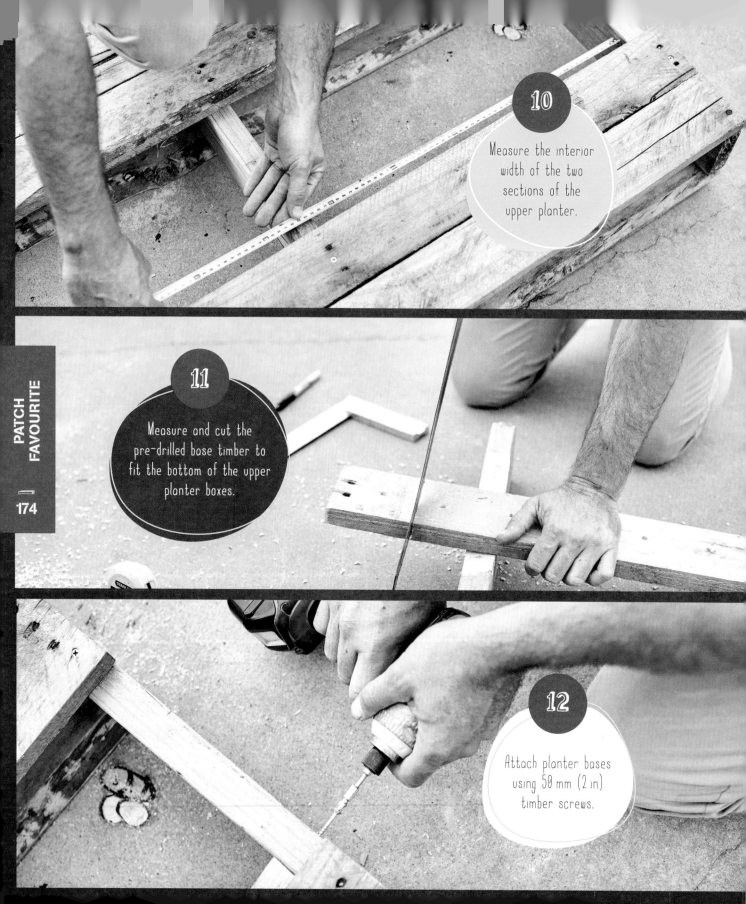

10 Measure the interior width of the two sections of the upper planter.

11 Measure and cut the pre-drilled base timber to fit the bottom of the upper planter boxes.

12 Attach planter bases using 50 mm (2 in) timber screws.

13

This pallet has no doubt been living on the streets for a while, so take a sander to it and smooth away those **ROUGHER EDGES**.

Fix an L-bracket at the top of each side of the pallet. Use some 50 mm (2 in) bulge head screws, as this will be weight bearing.

14 ›

‹ 15

You may consider using a food-safe plastic to line the inside of each planter box to increase the longevity of the unit (fix with staples or nails). Note: this can be tricky as space to work with your tools is very limited. The lining should still have drainage holes at the bottom. Otherwise, it will soon be full of stagnant soil and rotten plants.

16

Find a strong and handsome friend to help lift the wall garden while you attach it to the wall. Use 50 mm (2 in) bulge head screws for maximum security.

Fill planter boxes with premium organic potting mix. Depending on how high the wall garden is mounted, you may need a ladder to properly reach everything.

17 ⟩

⟨ 18

Plant out using some of our wall gardening favourites (see page 192). Plants with **SHALLOW ROOT DEPTH** tend to do the best, so think leafy greens, strawberries and herbs.

19 Water in your new plants. Daily watering is a very important part of maintaining a wall garden.

I've got 99 problems, but this **PALLET** ain't one.

PROJECT DETAILS

TIME 🕐

DIFFICULTY RATING 🥄

BUDGET 💰 💰

THINGS YOU'LL NEED...

- spare sunlit wall
- 3 x lengths of guttering
- drill set
- roofing silicone
- 3 x left gutter end
- 3 x right gutter end
- pencil
- string
- measuring tape
- 9 x gutter brackets
- 25 x 25 mm (1 in) timber screws
- premium potting mix
- lettuce seedlings
- water

RAIN GUTTER WALL GARDEN

GUTTERS YOU DON'T HAVE TO CLEAN OUT

One of the challenges of building a wall garden is finding materials that make construction straightforward, even for the lay handyperson. We do know people who enlist help to change over that tricky light globe, so if we want those same people growing food in what can often be the only sunlit spaces available, we need a system that is beyond simplistic.

Legend has it that the inventor of the rain gutter wall garden was a lazy man, who was simply tired of being asked to clean out the overflowing gutters on his spare weekend. Ultimately, the sight of weeds sprouting along the roofline was the trigger for great innovation. It inspired a gutter that intentionally grew things inside it, that didn't need to be cleaned out. Enter a new style of wall garden.

While the use of guttering to grow food is, without doubt, the creation of a man who went to great lengths to avoid work, ironically the use of the material has its limitations, meaning upkeep on the system is heightened. As is often the case with wall gardens, the mandatory shallow planting depths dictate what plants can and cannot be grown. It also means that you have to elevate your level of care so that they flourish.

The shallow depth of this material, approximately 150 mm (6 in), makes it suitable only for the most shallow-rooted annual plants – almost exclusively leafy greens. So it's quick-growing, snatch-and-grab-style lettuces. Rocket, mizuna, butterhead, the chois – pak and bok – will all do well in the rain gutter wall garden.

And so it didn't work out too badly for our innovator. Despite being a rather lazy man, he was rewarded with plenty of fresh garden salads.

1

Identify the best growing position for this wall garden. We want a wall that receives **GOOD SUNLIGHT** – preferably one that gathers the gentler morning rays.

>>

‹ 2

Old guttering isn't sturdy enough to hold a few wet old leaves, let alone soil and plants, so new guttering is best. Drill lots of drainage holes in the base of the guttering. You will be giving your gutters plenty of water to help the salads grow, so it's important that it drains well. Use a 10–15 mm (½ in) bit to prevent soil from falling out the bottom.

Use roofing silicone (available in any hardware store) to attach the ends of each gutter. This will keep soil from spilling out the sides. It's best to do this early so that the silicone has time to set.

3 ›

4

Decide the height at which you want to place the topmost gutter. Opinions differ, but it should be accessible from the ground.

5

Use a pencil to mark the placement of the first gutter bracket.

6

Use a string line to extrapolate the measurement out to the side. Mark the other end bracket.

7

Find the centre point with measuring tape and mark the placement of a middle bracket.

»

8 Attach gutter brackets with 25 mm (1 in) timber screws. Have a look at the opposite side of the fence to make sure that you haven't created a hazard for your neighbours.

9 Because we're growing salad greens, the gutters can be positioned relatively close, allowing just enough height for mature plants. Attach the next gutter 200–300 mm (8–12 in) below the first, and repeat for the third level.

10 Secure gutters in place by bending the metal tabs over the edge. That's right. Bend that metal with your bare hands. **DIY TO THE MAX!**

‹ 11

Fill the gutters with good-quality potting mix. We always say not to scrimp on quality, but particularly so when the depth of the planters is limited. Your lettuces will need all the help they can get.

12

Plant out your seedlings and give them a good watering. The design of potting mix makes it impossible to overwater in the presence of good drainage, so soak the gutter until water begins to **CASCADE** from the holes.

PROJECT DETAILS

184

TIME

DIFFICULTY RATING

BUDGET

THINGS YOU'LL NEED...

- felt pocket wall garden unit (found at most nurseries)
- wooden dowel
- drill set
- 2 x 50 mm (2 in) bulge head screws
- measuring tape
- 4 x cyprus timber lengths: 3 m x 70 mm/19 mm (9 ft 10 in x 2¾ in/¾ in)
- circular saw
- 25 x 40 mm (1½ in) timber screws
- 4 x 90° flat joining brackets
- 12 x 15 mm (½ in) timber screws
- 2 x large L-brackets
- good-quality organic potting mix
- favourite small-space plants

FRAMED POCKET WALL GARDEN

PICTURE PERFECT

Everything looks better framed. Those childhood drawings you did? Frame them. Those eyeballs in your head? Frame them. Old travel photos with a finger partially covering the lens? Frame them. Roger Rabbit, who framed him? I could go on and on. The point is that framing something just adds a little extra quality. Consider, for example, the trim on a window or cornices in a room. It is an easy way to add finish and polish to just about anything.

This same idea also applies to the garden. After all, what is a raised garden bed other than a glorified 3D frame that holds food? Defined boundaries make things look cleaner, more deliberate and solid. We've discovered that building a basic frame is a nice and easy way to glam up a wall garden by making it into a true feature.

Not all wall gardening units are created equal. While many may function the same, it generally seems that the more you are willing to spend, the more aesthetically pleasing the design will be. Of course, being a resourceful gardener means that such things should not trouble you. You make your own beauty in the world! Case in point is the felt pocket wall garden. These units are about the least expensive option in the prefabricated market and are simple to set up. However, their flaccid, listless shape does not inspire thoughts of gardening potency. Adding a frame will help to obscure the frumpy edges and turns this practical and affordable wall gardening solution into a feature.

1

Remove your pocket wall garden unit from the packaging and **READ THE INSTRUCTIONS**. Units should come with all of the hardware needed to mount to a wall. If this is not the case, buy some additional screws and washers for mounting.

2

This particular pocket garden has room to fit a wooden dowel along the top. Never ones to miss an opportunity, we will oblige.

3

Drill a leader hole at each end of the dowel, as you don't want to split the wood when you mount it to the wall.

Position your pocket garden where it will get plenty of sun. Use a couple of 50 mm (2 in) bulge head screws to mount the felt planter to the wall. It should now hang like a beautiful **PERSIAN TAPESTRY**.

< 4

Measure the dimensions of the wall garden, bearing in mind that you want the frame to cover the edges. In this case, our felt pocket planter is 1.2 m by 800 mm (3 ft 11 in by 2 ft 7½ in).

5 >

Measure and cut the timber into two lengths of 1.2 m (3 ft 11 in) and two widths of 800 mm (2 ft 7½ in). This will make up the frame that sits behind the capping.

< 6

7

Drill leader holes and join the frame together at the ends using 40 mm (1½ in) timber screws.

8

Doublecheck the length of the frame. Depending on how it is joined it will be slightly larger than the felt planter. Our frame is 1.2 m (3 ft 11 in).

9

Cut two 1.2 m (3 ft 11 in) lengths and place them on the top and bottom of the frame as capping.

»

‹ 10

Rather than doing some gnarly calculations to figure out the width minus the thickness of the two lengths, just measure the gap and cut your remaining two timber widths to size accordingly.

11

Attach four 90° joining brackets to connect each corner of the capping, using 15 mm (½ in) timber screws. It will be **A BIT WOBBLY,** but once mounted to the frame that won't matter.

‹ 12

Place the capping over the frame. Don't fret if it overhangs a little bit. That just adds extra **STYLE POINTS.**

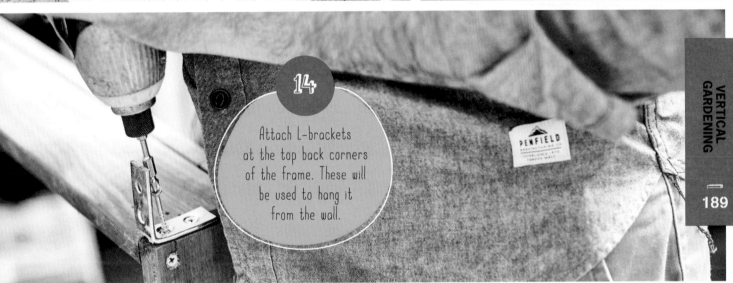

13 Secure the copping with 40 mm (1½ in) timber screws on each corner. Again, leader holes will prevent splitting here.

14 Attach L-brackets at the top back corners of the frame. These will be used to hang it from the wall.

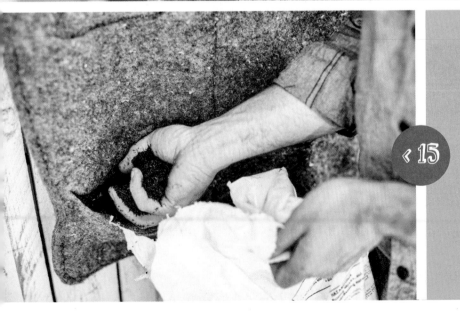

15 Fill the pocket wall garden with a high-quality organic potting mix. With so little soil, it really makes a difference to use the **BEST SOIL** available.

16

Plant out the wall garden with your favourite **SMALL SPACE VARIETIES.**

Mount the frame over the pocket garden using some 40 mm (1½ in) timber screws. As with all wall mounting systems, you need to make sure that you know what's on the other side, ensuring you aren't creating sharp hazards for your beloved neighbour.

‹ 17

TOP 5

VERTICAL GARDEN GOODIES TO GROW

The vertical garden is the best thing to happen to walls since Boston ivy. Unlike Boston ivy, however, edible plants won't slowly erode the masonry or leave you with a slimy pile of leaves. Some edible plants can provide year-round staples without taking up any ground space. The trick is picking the right ones.

1 STRAWBERRIES

These little red gems are the sweets (candy) of the gardening world. They can still give you a pretty good belly ache if you eat a lot, but overindulgence is fraught with a lot less guilt than eating a bag of Party Mix by yourself. Strawberries are a great treat to have on demand, and are well suited to the wall life. Most importantly, they have shallow roots that creep out rather than dig deep to find water, which is perfect for the shallow soil depths of most wall gardening units. Strawberries will continuously send runners to expand coverage, which will result in a wall garden that is densely packed with delicious treats. Go ahead, have another!

Leafy greens have shallow root systems and are absolutely dying to be picked. The best way to keep leafy greens healthy is to continuously harvest them and the best way to do that is to have them at eye level. Planting a large variety of greens such as English spinach, iceberg lettuce, boston lettuce, rocket (arugula) and radicchio will not only ensure that you have variety on your plate, but will also help to create a wall garden that is rich in texture and colour. Keep in mind that salad greens are not as hardy as other plants and a little extra water will go a long way. Just like in the ground patch, wind and heat can easily stress these plants so make sure they are watered every morning and you will have a happy, healthy salad to pick when you get home from work.

2 MIXED SALADS

3
THYME

This perennial herb is the perfect care-free wall garden plant owing to its shallow root depth and hardy nature. Unlike coriander (cilantro), parsley or basil, which require a lot of attention, thyme likes a little bit of tough love and won't bolt to flower if you forget to water it for a couple of days. It understands that you are a busy person with lots of things to do and that when you do have your time together it will be meaningful. Thyme is that old reliable friend that you may only catch up with once a month, but you don't feel like you ever miss a beat. It will be there for you when that ragu is missing a certain x-factor or when you need something special for your marinating goat's cheese. Yes, thyme and thyme again.

This should come as no surprise to fans of the Little Veggie Patch Co – we [expletive] love tomatoes and will grow them anywhere. The challenge with growing tomatoes in a wall garden is getting enough soil depth. However, if you do have a little extra depth, or perhaps are using hanging milk crates, growing hanging tomatoes can be a rewarding endeavour. As far as I can tell, tomatoes were never meant to grow up in the first place. We have created a whole elaborate industry of trellis and twine so that we can support a plant that by all accounts just wants to fall over. Let the tomato be its lazy self and spill down walls like hanging grapes at a Dionysian bathhouse. Now, all you need is a pair of nymphs to dangle the tomatoes into your mouth while you play a merry tune on the lute.

4
TOMATOES

5
NASTURTIUM

These hearty, self-seeding flowers are a patch favourite and a wall garden hero. Nasturtiums are nearly impossible to kill and will come back year after year, creating a cascade of green, yellow and red down even the most average of walls. Like a vintage soul and funk record store, growing nasturtiums will attract the coolest crowd in town (of insects that is), so prepare for visitors. But you are not just growing nasturtiums to look cool and attract pollinators – nasturtiums are delightfully edible, too. The leaves pack a strong, sharp, peppery punch while the flowers provide a mellow sweet kiss to the palate. Nasturtium is one of those rare cases where substance and beauty come together. Don't let this one get away.

PROJECT LIST

GARDEN
BASICS

We know that many of you may have come on the journey with us so far – right from our humble beginnings as two guys pretending that we knew what we were doing, to the modern-day Little Veggie Patch Co (the wise institution of growing food we are today). While this book is mostly tailored to the dedicated followers who want to take this growing caper to the next step, we will never discount the value of including the newbies, and so it's important to recap the 101s.

This chapter also gives us the opportunity to remember the good old days, when veggie-patching life was simple and straightforward – the days when it was all about the vegetables, and there was nothing beyond growing the tastiest, ripest tomatoes on the vine. It's a trip down memory lane, through all the fundamental elements of growing food, and the absolute essential DIYs that continue to be worth their weight in tomatoes.

Over the years we have certainly evolved and refined some of our techniques, but the outcome remains the same. It's all about creating the right infrastructure for growing food – like the initial set-up of the patch stalwart, the raised garden bed. This is the one that brings all the old times rushing back. The smell of quality cypress pine, angling for warm cuppas from our clients and that feeling at the end of the day that you've really accomplished something.

Then we revisit all the helpers that run alongside and support the patch. There's the ultimate compost machine, which keeps the beds well fed and productive; and the irrigation system, which is more reliable and efficient than the saintliest next-door neighbour. We also return to the relationship between a fruit tree and the garden. It's one that can be life-long, meaningful and truly productive.

Sometimes the simple things truly are the best and an uncomplicated, coherent, well-organised patch can be so satisfying and rewarding. That is where we began at the Little Veggie Patch Co, and we've been lucky enough to see our business grow and develop to where it is today. It's really all about getting the simple things done right. For that reason it feels only fitting to run through them again – with some slight twists – one more time.

PROJECT DETAILS

TIME

DIFFICULTY RATING

BUDGET

THINGS YOU'LL NEED...

- rake
- tape measure
- pencil
- 8 x cypress pine lengths:
  3.6 m x 200 mm/38 mm
  (11 ft 9½ in x 8 in/1½ in)
- circular saw
- 100 x 70 mm (2¾ in) bulge head
  screws
- drill set
- spirit level

BUILDING A RAISED VEGGIE PATCH

THE GOOD OL' DAYS

There was once a time when the world of the Little Veggie Patch Co (LVPC) only featured the raised garden bed – and cups of tea in between. A typical day would entail a trip to the timber yard for some 38 mm (1½ in) cypress pine beauties, a trip to Bunnings for some 75 mm (3 in) baton screws, and a return trip home because we had forgotten the drill.

It was a world that in itself was quite worldly, because the early days of LVPC was a melting pot of cultures that came together and built raised garden beds. The first person to get involved was a passionate travelling Frenchman by the name of Sylvain. He was my first veggie patch soulmate, and co-creator of the business, and I look back on those early, organic days with great fondness. We built a garden bed, had a cup of tea, and then we moved on to the next.

With the raised garden bed front and centre, life was so uncomplicated. Our style of edible gardening was more broadly based on the themes of permaculture back then. Larger spaces, more interaction between the elements, a more complete cyclical system. Along with a garden bed, there may be some fruit trees, a composting system, and the notion that perhaps one day the owners would get off the grid.

Since then we have pulled away from traditional permaculture because one of its basic ideas is to take what you have got, and then improve it. But how can you take a slab of concrete on the 35th floor and use it to grow plants? A business evolution has led us to smaller and even smaller space gardening, and that's the place we find ourselves now.

Of course, if you have room for a raised garden bed, it's still the perfect infrastructure for growing food. For us, it also gives us the chance to reminisce about the good ol' days.

1

Before starting the construction, it is important to make the site for your garden bed completely **LEVEL**. Use a rake to make a flat pad. This will make the entire process sooooo much easier. Make sure you spend a bit of time getting this part right, removing any weeds and grasses in the process.

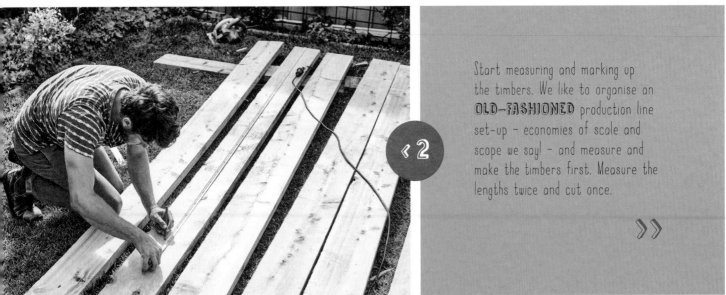

2

Start measuring and marking up the timbers. We like to organise on **OLD-FASHIONED** production line set-up – economies of scale and scope we say! – and measure and make the timbers first. Measure the lengths twice and cut once.

»

Cut your timbers. For the bed we want to build, we need six 2.4 m (7 ft 10½ in) lengths, six 1.5 m (4 ft 11 in) widths and ten 600 mm (1 ft 11½ in) uprights/braces. When cutting, it helps not to force the circular saw through too quickly. Give it time to cut and let it go at its own speed. You will get **STRAIGHTER CUTS** and everything will slot together more nicely. That will give us more reasons to celebrate with **CUPS OF TEA**.

‹ 3

Start by affixing the two lengths of the garden bed in slabs of three 2.4 m (7 ft 10½ in) lengths, braced together by three 600 mm (1 ft 11½ in) uprights. Lie lengths down with an end brace underneath. The end brace should extend beyond the lengths by the exact thickness of the timber (38 mm/1½ in). Size up using another timber length. It will make sense later.

4 ›

5

As well as the two end uprights that are overhanging the thickness of the timber, attach a centre upright for extra rigidity.

‹ 6

Now it's time to begin construction. Start by taking an entire length slab and nestle it into position. Use the spirit level to make sure it is completely level horizontally and vertically, and affix one 1.5 m (4 ft 11 in) width piece at ground level to hold it in place.

Build it up with two more pieces and you have half the unit complete. If we were cutting with robot precision and using timber of the exact same grade and thickness, adding the remaining pieces would result in a perfect fit first time, but this is **WOODWORK**, and we consider ourselves **IMPERFECT**.

7 ›

‹ 8

Because it's very difficult to achieve perfection first time round, you may need to **TEST-BUILD** before screwing in. You can then chock the bottom one up or slightly dig it in to make it fit. Once happy, screw together using two 70 mm (2¾ in) bulge head screws for each piece of timber.

››

9

Next comes the opposing side. Muscle it into position and attach it, ensuring it is level all over. **TEA TIME** perhaps? Nope, attach the remaining widths first and then put on a brew.

10

The remaining uprights help to cover any blemishes or fixes that you've made along the way. Attach them at the four corners of the bed. To hold these uprights in place, use a couple of 70 mm (2¾ in) bulge head screws from the inside of the bed. That way your bed exterior will be screw-free, and you'll have a **PERFECTLY CRAFTED** raised garden bed (with all blemishes classily hidden).

PROJECT DETAILS

TIME

DIFFICULTY
RATING

BUDGET

THINGS YOU'LL NEED...

- plastic rubbish bin or bucket, with lid
- handsaw
- drill set
- 2 x 15 mm (½ in) screws
- bracket
- shovel
- compost or potting mix
- tiger worms
- vegetable food scraps

WORM PLUNGER
BUILD IT AND THEY WILL COME

Conventional worm farms and composting bins are plagued by a few problems. For one, they can be unsightly, hulking objects that take up valuable garden real estate. Another issue is that pests easily infiltrate them. A lot of compost bins are open at the bottom, which means that any motivated rat with a little initiative need only to dig a couple of centimetres to reach a sumptuous vegetarian buffet.

Such nefarious activity was, in fact, a cultural highlight in a previous sharehouse. There, my housemates and I used to gather around the kitchen window every evening and watch a pair of rat bachelors fight it out for nightly control of the compost bin. Oh, how I miss Scabs and Snaggletooth ...

Rather than building rat colosseums we prefer to build worm apartments, and so the idea for the worm plunger was born. A worm plunger is nothing more than a plastic bin or bucket buried underground, which, so I've heard, is where worms like to live. We drill holes in the walls of the plunger to facilitate movement and it has a cap, which can be removed to add compost.

While this system is smaller than a conventional worm farm, it has the benefit of being both discreet and difficult to infiltrate. The added benefit of being underground is that temperatures are normalised so worms will be at their most productive. Once it's full, you can either remove and spread the worm castings around your patch or simply slide the bucket out of the ground and move the infrastructure to another part of the garden.

< 1 Start by finding a suitable place in your patch to **COLONISE.** The worms will drastically improve the soil quality in the area so try a particularly unproductive area in need of reinvigoration. This unit can be thought of as an overflow when your compost bin is full – or the primary unit if you are particularly strapped for space, or if rats are a genuine concern.

Any old bin or bucket will do, provided it has a lid. We found this plastic bucket at the shops and it looks like it was purpose-built for our cause. Start by sawing off the bottom. **2 >**

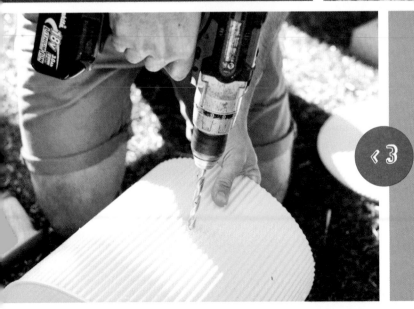

< 3 Drill plenty of holes into the sides of the bucket. These will be entryways for the occupants of this **UNDERGROUND CITY.** Studies of urban transportation systems have shown that improving service is the only way to increase usage of public transport, so ensure there are enough holes so no worm has to queue for too long.

>>

4 Screw a bracket to the lid to make a **SIMPLE HANDLE**.

5 Dig a hole just deep enough that the lid will sit flush with ground level. Place the bucket in the hole and backfill the area around it. There will inevitably be leftover soil, so find a home for it elsewhere in the garden.

‹6 Transfer a small amount of existing compost into the bottom of the new system. If you don't have any existing compost, a few handfuls of potting mix will do. Until they build up some good soil, the worms will need a comfortable place to **RETREAT** into when they are not eating your kitchen waste.

Add in the tiger worms. They are solitary, sensitive creatures but, as the name suggests, these stripey fellas are also **FEROCIOUS EATERS**.

8

Once the worms are in place, it is time to begin your **COMPOSTING OPERATION** in earnest. Almost all vegetarian food scraps can go into the plunger except for citrus peels and avocados, and not too much onion and garlic.

BON APPÉTIT!

PATCH FAVOURITE

PROJECT DETAILS

TIME

DIFFICULTY RATING

BUDGET

THINGS YOU'LL NEED...

- split-line head
- teflon tape
- battery timer
- 9V battery
- 13 mm (½ in) director
- 13 mm (½ in) black poly tubing
- packet of 13 mm (½ in) clamps
- locking or multi grip pliers
- pipe cutters
- packet of tees
- drill set
- packet of elbows
- 13 mm (½ in) drip hose
- tent pegs
- small screw
- 2-way director
- 4 mm black poly tubing
- spike dripper

IRRIGATING THE PATCH

LEAN ON YOUR NEIGHBOUR FOR BUTTER RATHER THAN WATERING DUTIES

Without water your garden will NOT survive your extended holiday down at the beach house. And it will battle when you take the kids skiing in the mountains for a week in July. While we are fortunate to live in a country where we can grow things all year round, that blessing does not extend to rainfall and there's little chance the big guy upstairs will fix things when you're too busy.

The fallback option – your next-door neighbour – should only ever be that, because frequent holidays and favours will soon harshly test that relationship. It's time to take some responsibility and get organised.

As busy people, we're realistic about the time constraints of modern life – you may even struggle to keep up with Instagram these days – so it's important to lean on all the tools that modern life has to offer. One of those is an irrigation system.

An irrigation system is superior to the perfect neighbour because it will water when they would often be asleep, and it can do it through a drip hose, which administers water directly to the plants' roots. That is where the plant needs and uses water, so why not be obliging? Avoiding wet leaf foliage – the by-product of traditional, inefficient watering systems – means less chance of disease and pest attacks. And by traditional, inefficient systems I mean you standing there with a beer in one hand and the garden hose in the other.

The limitation of irrigation has always been installation. But in much the same way as certain industries heighten the difficulty of their job to protect their business, irrigation specialists are guilty of overhyping the task at hand. A drip system is an easily achievable DIY activity, and it will help remove the most volatile element that determines the success of your veggie patch. You watering!

The most complicated part of any system is attaching it to the mains water. This, in itself, is a job for a plumber. Note that by having full pressure running through your system, it can cause many issues, such as bits popping off. For this set-up, we come off the tap but attach a split-line head so that one line will service your hose and the other this system.

< 1

Whenever you have a join that requires **THREADING**, make sure to loop teflon tape over the thread to help seal the join.

2 >

Now, attach a battery timer to one line. A simple timer like this is inexpensive, runs on a single 9V battery and can be set up to four stages of **WATERING TIMES**. To put it simply, it's everything that you need and nothing you don't.

< 3

>>

< 4

Set your timer to your required watering times. This will depend on the time of year and the maturity of your plants. Rather than have us trying to explain how to set the timer, reference the **INSTRUCTIONS**. They will, no doubt, make a lot more sense.

5

Screw in a director on the end of the timer to which you'll attach your 13 mm (½ in) black poly.

< 6

Attach one end of your 13 mm (½ in) black poly to the director. Note that the poly tubing comes coiled and can be difficult to work with when constructing small grids. Try unwinding them and laying them in the sun – the plastic softens and the lines become far easier to use.

Whenever you make a join, use clamps (tightened with locking or multi grip pliers) to hold each join in place. Without the clamps there is the potential for the fittings to burst apart under **PRESSURE**, and you'll be watering the corner of the house rather than the garden while you're away.

‹ 7

Now feed this line to the place in your garden that requires water. The line is pretty **MALLEABLE** and can be curved around obstacles, but if going around sharp corners, it's best to insert an elbow. Bury the line under soil or grass where possible. Irrigation is a **DOG'S FAVOURITE**.

8 ›

9

To feed your water into your crates or sections of garden, make a cut and insert a 'T' piece.

››

‹ 10

With the 'T' in, water can go to the crate and then continue to other parts of the garden. Ensure you clamp at this point.

11

For the hose to feed into the crate, DRILL a hole at the soil height. It needs to be a little bigger than the 13 mm (½ in) black poly.

‹ 12

Continue the 13 mm (½ in) black poly up to the entrance hole and insert an elbow and a little more black poly to enter your patch.

‹ 13

Now it's time to move onto the 14 mm (½ in) drip hose. This is usually made of brown plastic and has a hole every 300 mm (12 in) that releases 2–3 litres (68–101 fl oz or 8–12 cups) of water an hour. Putting this together is easy. Just make sure you cut the pipe at least 30 mm (1¼ in) from a drip. Too close and it will affect the connections.

Because the hose has been coiled for a long time it can be a pain to cut pieces. The hose flattens out when uncoiled, weighted down and laid out in the sunshine.

14 ›

‹ 15

Start creating your grid of drip irrigation. Lines should be **SPACED OUT** every 300 mm (12 in) to match the spacing of the drips on the hose.

16 > Once you have your grids set up and secured with clamps, use tent pegs to hold the drip hose on the soil. This can then be covered over with mulch when it's time.

If you want to water an individual pot near the grid, you can attach 4 mm tubing and an individual dripper. Start by piercing the drip tubing with a small screw.

17 >

18 Push in a two-way director to which the 4 mm tubing will be attached.

19

Attach the tubing and feed it to the pot.

Finally, attach a spike dripper. These have a nozzle on them that **REGULATES** the flow of water and will need to be adjusted when you test the system. Remember, the drip hose valves release 2–3 litres (68–101 fl oz or 8–12 cups) per hour, but these spike drippers will release the same quantity per minute if left fully open.

20 ›

‹ 21

TEST the system. Check for leaks and poor seals. Check for clamps that are not tight. Reduce the flow of the spike drippers. When all that is done, book some flights, sort out accommodation and let the next-door neighbour know you're off again.

PROJECT DETAILS

TIME

DIFFICULTY RATING

BUDGET

THINGS YOU'LL NEED...

- 10 long bamboo stakes
- sturdy twine
- peas or beans (depending on the season)
- passionfruit (for perennial hiding)
- water

CLIMBING TEEPEE
A PLACE TO CALL THEIR OWN

When I was a kid one of my favourite books was *The Secret Garden* by Francis Hodgson Burnett. As I remember it, an orphaned girl is sent to live with her stodgy uncle in a large old English estate. She discovers a locked and hidden garden, which becomes her private world and a source of wonderment and joy. There were, no doubt, a lot of heavy themes that were largely lost on me at the time, but what still remains is the idea of exploration and a secret place that is all your own.

To say that kids love forts, cubby houses or any other type of hideout is a grievous understatement. It is a private place just for them. It is a place where they make the rules and others have to follow. Oh, and boy do kids like making rules – almost as much as we adults do. I'm meant to be a grown man and the idea of a tree fort still sounds great to me. Sometimes the hardest part of being an adult is having to pretend that you are more mature than a five-year-old laughing at their own farts. So why fight it? Build a climbing teepee and let the kids make the rules.

The climbing teepee is a sort of glorified trellis system that gradually becomes a secret hideout as climbing plants ascend the supports. Peas and beans are the perfect plants, as they are fearless climbers and will cover the structure in a few short months. The best part of this teepee is that there will always be fresh, healthy food on tap. After all, if I learned anything from *Charlie and the Chocolate Factory* it is that the only thing better than a magical world is a magical world that you can eat.

‹ 1 Start by finding a suitable location for this new settlement. There are a lot of factors to consider, such as the proximity to food resources, water supply and hostile neighbours.

Grab some snacks and discuss the location in depth. Talk about **EXPANSION PLANS**, but be realistic about zoning in your neighbourhood. Is the property heritage-listed? **2 ›**

‹ 3 Submit a building permit to council and wait for the appropriate authorisation before starting any new construction on your property.

Once you have permission from the correct authority, clear the land and bury the end of the bamboo stakes in a wide circle. Steel-cap boots, high-vis and hardhats are essential. Safety saves lives, mate.

‹ 4

Pull the bamboo together at the top and tie tightly with **STURDY** twine. The structure should really be looking like a teepee now. Make sure that there is a large-enough opening on one side to be turned into an entrance.

5 ›

Once the basic structure is in place, plant some climbers at the base of each pole. Beans and peas are excellent seasonal options, and scarlet runner beans are a great perennial choice. For a long-term investment, try passionfruit.

‹ 6

Water your seeds regularly until germinated and, as with most edibles, continue to water them every morning. This should most certainly be the responsibility of the young explorers. In time, the teepee should be covered and ready for their rules.

PROJECT DETAILS

TIME

DIFFICULTY RATING

BUDGET

THINGS YOU'LL NEED...

- lovely sunny position
- fruit tree of choice
- shovel
- organic slow-release fertiliser
- watering can (and water)
- bag of compost
- 2 stakes
- axe, hammer or mallet
- soft twine
- pea straw, sugar cane mulch or lucerne hay

PLANTING A FRUIT TREE
A LIFE-LONG ROMANCE

A fruit tree is a friend for life. More than that, it is a friend for many lifetimes. The fruit trees you see gnarled, twisted and scarred – the good old boys and girls at the neighbour's house – have been around for decades. Just like Frank or Rita or Vicky, who all rode the wave of immigration in the 1950s, these fruit trees came along with them. It was like bringing something familiar from home, an old friend, to help them assimilate to a new life.

If given the chance, they will outlive us all – and even decades on, they don't need much help. The trees that have survived and then flourished in their new environment become trees for life. Overhanging laneways or footpaths, offering a glut of fruit each season, these are simply old friends that will always have a lot to offer.

Each tree that you plant in the garden has the potential to be another friend for life. It is an opportunity to give something back to your neighbourhood and to the land that you won't live on forever. Or, if you're possessive, a tree can be planted in a pot and live a good transient life, too, keeping you company as you move.

Getting into such a relationship means a serious level of commitment, and that commitment needs to be applied when planting your new BFF. Following a simple set of rules from day one will set you on the right path. And that could determine whether this ends up a life-long bond or just a fleeting romance.

‹ 1

When you are making important commitments like this, don't save the best position in your garden in case another, better-looking fruit tree comes into your life. Live for the now and make this the one; choose a sunny space with good airflow.

First, you will need to dig a hole. We like to dig it much bigger than the root ball of the fruit tree. Loosening up the soil around the root ball will make early root growth much easier, when the plant isn't so strong. Dig a hole that is twice its depth and width.

2 ›

3

Throw in a handful of slow release organic fertiliser. This will help build up soil **FERTILITY.**

››

Now, fill the hole with water and let it dissipate through the soil. This will ensure the plant is more receptive to water as it establishes, and will assist the **EARLY ROOT GROWTH** into that harder zone.

< **4**

Partly backfill the hole with a mix of the loose soil and the bag of compost, so that it is now the depth of the root ball.

5 >

< **6**

It's time to prepare the tree for planting. Inspect for forked or twisted roots. These are signs that the plant has been in the pot for too long and will really be looking forward to this new life. Cut out any forked roots and **UNTANGLE** those that go around and around and around.

Position the plant in the hole and backfill with the mix of soil and more compost. Make sure you compact the soil around the tree and don't have any coming up its trunk.

< 7

8

Now, apply a little more slow release organic fertiliser, and water in thoroughly. The tree will need plenty of water as it **ESTABLISHES** – depending on what time of year you're planting, it could be almost daily.

>>

STAKE either side of the tree, keeping away from the root zone to avoid damage. Have a think about whether there are irrigation or stormwater/sewage pipes before you go bashing in your stakes!

< 9

10

Tie twine to one stake and then around the tree. Repeat with the other stake. Now your new friend is secure.

< 11

The final step is **MULCHING**. Use pea straw, sugar cane mulch or lucerne hay, and mulch to a depth of 5 cm (2 in).

PROJECT DETAILS

TIME

DIFFICULTY RATING

BUDGET

THINGS YOU'LL NEED...

- secateurs
- paper bags
- glass jars with lids
- texta (marker)
- knife and spoon
- sieve
- water
- bowl or plate

SEED SAVING
LIVING LEGENDS

Sometimes the garden really goes out of its way to grab your attention, particularly at the end or beginning of the hot months. Great conical towers of lettuce suddenly appear in the patch along with bouquets of white, red, purple, yellow and blue. Every other colour imaginable is suddenly on show, along with a lot of ratty dying tendrils. It's as if the garden is trying to tell you something, leaning out of its chair and putting its hand up to say, 'Pick me! Pick me! Pick me!' The plants are essentially giving themselves over to you. Who do you think you are, trying to deny them?

In fact, 'pick me' is exactly what the garden is trying to tell you. It's the end of the growing season and time to start thinking ahead. Seed saving is an essential part of gardening and, over time, is what makes your garden truly your own. Take inventory of what you've got. Make a note of what worked and what failed. Think about what you would try again. Every season is an opportunity to do things better and that starts with choosing the right seeds.

Everything we buy from the market tastes, looks or feels how it does because of human selection. Our plants are just as domesticated as our animals and a lot of great varieties have been lost for the convenience of storage or rate of growth. Conventional tomatoes are red because someone determined that is what consumers now expect. Fortunately, there are still a lot of heirloom seeds that will deliver more charismatic produce. Seed saving is essentially starting your own heirloom seed legacy. Every season you can slowly work your way towards the produce that you want. Whether you select for taste, size, hardiness or colour, seed saving is not only a way to get more out of the patch, it will also save quite a bit of money in the long run.

Seeds generally come from a plant's fruit or the seed head that develops after the plant goes to flower. Take the time to figure out what you are dealing with. Generally speaking, leafy greens, root vegetables and the brassicas go to flower and then form seed heads, whereas plants like tomatoes, pumpkins, zucchini and cucumber will have seeds inside. If you haven't already noticed, bean and pea pods contain tasty seeds, too.

‹ 1

2

Once your plant has developed **SEED PODS**, trim them and hang them out to dry.

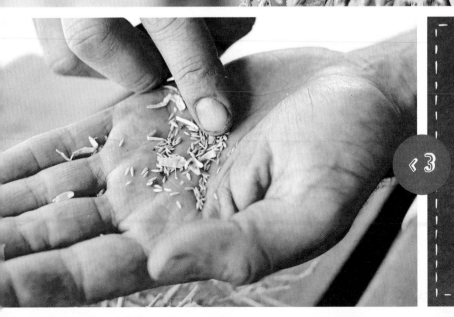

‹ 3

Once the seed pods have dried, you should be able to free up a lot of seeds by putting the pods in a paper bag and simply shaking the bag or crushing the flower heads with your fingers. Plant material will fall apart, but the seeds will be hard and strong. This is known as **THRESHING**

‹ 4

Store seeds in an airtight jar. **LABEL** with the year, variety and any other relevant information. Store in a cool, dark place.

Plants such as zucchini, tomato and cucumber require a slightly different process, but the basic idea is the same. Separate the seeds, dry them out and store them. Take a cucumber, for example. Begin by slicing a cucumber in half. Scrape the soft flesh and seeds out of the fruit and transfer them to a sieve for separation.

5 ›

‹ 6

Place the sieve under a tap and run water through the flesh while gently massaging the seeds. Eventually all of the soft bits will wash through the sieve, leaving only seeds behind.

« 7 Transfer the seeds to a bowl or plate and leave out to dry. After a day or two, scrape the seeds into a storage jar.

8 Label the jar and store in a cool, dry place, next to your other seed friends!

CUCUMBER GREEN GEM
·14/15

LETTUCE
2/3/15

PROJECT DETAILS

TIME

DIFFICULTY RATING

BUDGET

THINGS YOU'LL NEED...

- compost bin
- 700 mm (2 ft 3½ in) length of 90 mm (3½ in) PVC pipe
- handsaw
- drill and 10 mm (½ in) drill bit
- wooden stake or stick
- piece of wood
- hammer
- bag of 2000 worms (tiger or red worms)
- scraps – a good mix of brown and green waste

THE ULTIMATE COMPOST SET-UP
GET EVERYONE INVOLVED

It is hard bringing two very different worlds together. It's a bit like separate friendship groups. The idea can be so overwhelming that it's just easier to keep them apart. After all, why challenge something that is comfortable and that works fine?

Take your school group. These are people you lived with through adolescence and have shared all the details of your teenage relationships. Like the time you kissed your beloved on the nose by accident. You see, that's your common ground and something the work group wouldn't get. These days your awkwardness is much more mature and developed, and you've come a long way since kissing noses. But isn't it your awkwardness that's the common bond? Isn't there great value in comparing both old and new embarrassing stories?

Sometimes we can be blind to the value that comes from bringing things together. Much like your two friendship groups that work so well apart, the worm farm and compost bins alone are such efficient systems that there seems little to gain from bringing them together. But without challenge, there's no further gain, and by not introducing your friends you have missed the opportunity to create a super friendship group that can laugh at you. And in the case of the worm farm and compost bin, you could be missing out on the ultimate compost machine.

By adding worms to your compost bin, the worms are back-up for the more stubborn compost material the bin leaves behind. Or is it the other way around? What is certain is that together they will process your waste into useable, invaluable compost faster and that is not only beneficial to your veggie patch, but landfill piles around the country as well. Oh, and the worms and microbes will have their bellies full and be happy, too. Yes, everyone's a winner.

‹ 1

Place your compost bin. Some people think that bins should be placed in the sun to accelerate the heating of the pile, which then in turn creates the right environment for composting. But that is a fallacy – and your worms won't appreciate getting baked either. When choosing a space, keep it shaded and, for vanity's sake, out of the way.

2 ›

To lower the risk of turning your machine into a stinky pile of rubbish, a **BREATHER** pipe is a good idea. This ensures enough air gets through the scraps, which is important for both the worms and the microbes that create compost. Measure the height of your bin and cut your pipe 200 mm (8 in) longer.

3

Lay the pipe flat on the ground and cut to the desired length.

»

‹ 4

Drill plenty of holes, evenly or randomly, throughout the entire length of PVC. This will facilitate **AIRFLOW** through the compost heap and encourage aerobic processes that break down your scraps.

Use a wooden stake or stick to clear a hole at the centre of the compost. The hole should be about 200 mm (8 in), just big enough to hold the PVC pipe standing upright.

5 ›

6

Place a piece of wood on top of the **AERATOR** pipe and gently tap it down into place. Make sure the compost bin lid will still fit securely.

< 7

Once the bin is in action, set the **WORMS** free and let them join the party. To our shock and horror, everyone's having a good time. This is **FANTASTIC!** More scraps, more compost, more quickly ...

8

Start filling with scraps, remembering to get a good mix of brown and green waste. Despite the pipe and worms, it's still a good idea to **BALANCE** out the waste.

TOP 5

PEST MANAGEMENT TECHNIQUES

—

Everyone wants to know about pests and the best way to take them out. But rather than preoccupying yourself with warfare, sometimes the best approach is a peaceful one, simply letting them know that your patch is off-limits. In this top five, we show you how to walk the line of conflict and peace in modern pest warfare.

1
NETTING

(POSSUMS, WHITE CABBAGE MOTH, BIRDS, LAZY RATS)

A netting fortress around your patch is exactly that, and it will deter and prevent access for a number of the larger pests. Properly constructed netting – pulled taut and not hanging on plants as a climbing ladder – will keep out possums and birds. And if the rats in your vicinity are relatively lazy, they'll find it a big enough deterrent to go bother someone else. Finer netting, used over the patch when your seedlings are young and most attractive to the white cabbage moth, will deny landing space for the moths to lay their larvae. That's not to say they won't lay nearby and the caterpillars won't then crawl into the patch and start feasting, but it does set them back. See the number five technique if you inevitably encounter those fat green caterpillars in the patch.

(ALL PESTS) We've probably told you enough times by now that the open invitation for pests into your patch is when you water the garden nearing nightfall. Not only do plants go to sleep at night and take up little moisture then, but all pests – even those that don't dwell in the garden – head out to feed under the cover of darkness. Of course, an essential element is water, and having the patch moist at night helps push through the lovely fragrances and scents of everything growing in it. We know this will feel so wrong, but watering first thing in the morning, as part of the daily routine, will give your plants access to water when they need it, not the pests. To compound the effectiveness of your watering strategy, use a drip system that feeds water directly to the root zone or avoid randomly blasting each plant with the garden hose. Avoiding wet foliage further helps keep the night crawlers out of the patch.

2
WATERING

3
ECO-OIL

(WHITEFLY, APHIDS) Sucking pests, such as whitefly and aphids, are seasonal pests that go bonkers for early spring weather. The increase in heat, along with more frequent rainfall, creates a humid environment that these pests revel in. Rather than bemoan your horrible luck and take this influx personally, put a dent in their fun by hitting them early with a purpose-built spray, such as eco-oil. Old-school garlic sprays are also effective in this regard, but a more powerful potion, administered in a timely fashion – not on a ridiculously hot, sunny day, nor on a wet, rainy one – will help kill their vibe. One application is never enough, so build on the first spray by hitting them with another a few days later.

(ALL PESTS) We all know from experience that good hygiene helps entice the good things in life, and a lack of it attracts the bad – because you get the funk. The garden can also get its funk on if you drop the hygiene ball. Maintaining a clean garden is not a monumental task, and needs only a touch of grooming. Jobs include removing dead limbs/plants, mulching the patch, picking fruit when it's ready, culling plants that are growing over the top of each other, and giving the patch its bath in the morning. A clean and healthy patch means there's less food for the pests to feed on, and when the plants are strong, they are less susceptible to an outbreak of disease.

4
HYGIENE

5
DIPEL

(WHITE CABBAGE MOTH) Every veggie gardener needs to brace themselves for the inevitable visit from these nasty, green caterpillars, the offspring of this moth. The nature and numbers of the moth means that some of them, in some way, will eventually break through or outsmart your fortifications, so there will come a time when you come face to face with this old adversary. If the damage is minimal and numbers seem small, a game of search and destroy should be sufficient in controlling them. But when you find yourself overwhelmed, the fallback option is an organic spray known as Dipel, a naturally occurring bacteria that targets caterpillars. It's like a sniper that only takes out the target. The only problem is that the sniper can't identify between harmless and harmful caterpillars, so it is indiscriminate and will take out all caterpillars. Unfortunately, some collateral damage may sometimes be necessary for the greater good of your garden.

PROJECT LIST

PATCH FAVOURITE

TOP 5

As human beings we are constantly evolving, and the food we put into our bodies seems the greatest instigator of change. Eating more means we are getting bigger. But what type of bigger depends on the foods we throw down the hatch. Hopefully yours is not some sort of waste disposal unit (I'm certainly accused of that sometimes).

While we tend to eat more than we used to, the way we eat food remains relatively unchanged because our culinary repertoires are so entrenched. Tomatoes tend to go into the same salads, zucchinis in the same fritters, cucumbers the same delicious gin and tonics ... Yes, old habits die hard, and they die the hardest in the kitchen.

Bringing about change in the kitchen is difficult, because the kitchen is mostly a place of great comfort. I turn to the kitchen when everything else in life is complicated and off-kilter, and use it to revisit old recipes in an effort to restore balance. Finding the right kind of motivation for kitchen invention and experimentation is challenging, because impromptu kitchen chemistry can be messy. Of course, it's best if all final outcomes are palatable, but sometimes you need to create explosions to reap culinary reward.

The relationship between the patch and the kitchen is such an obvious one. The patch gives you the produce to create great culinary feats, and is the ultimate reward for all your hard work in the garden. Keeping a great patch is the motivation to cook great meals. And cooking great meals becomes the motivation to keep an even better patch. As you improve your repertoire, you will lift the meals that grace your kitchen table, but also the produce that goes into making them. Patch and kitchen are like the ultimate training partners – as one improves, it pulls the other one up to that new level.

The activities in this chapter revolve around all things food – preparation, preserving, cooking and seasonality. Throw yourself into each project – and get the kids involved, too. Spending time in the kitchen lab is something that is best started from a young age. Kids love getting involved, particularly when there is the potential to make a great mess. So, curb those instincts to keep your home tidy and pristine, and let the experimentation begin. The outcome could be great invention, and a whole new repertoire.

PATCH FAVOURITE

PROJECT DETAILS

TIME

DIFFICULTY RATING

BUDGET

THINGS YOU'LL NEED...

- large saucepan
- jars with lids
- 1–1.5 kg (2 lb 3 oz–3 lb 5 oz) beetroots (beets)
- 750 ml (25½ fl oz/3 cups) water
- 500 ml (17 fl oz/2 cups) white-wine vinegar
- 220 g (8 oz/1 cup) sugar
- pinch of salt
- medium saucepan
- mandoline
- ingredients per 500 ml (17 fl oz/2 cups) jar:
  - 1 tablespoon coriander seeds
  - 1 tablespoon mustard seeds
  - 4–5 cloves
  - 2 pieces lemon rind
- labels
- texta (marker)

EASY PRESERVING
NONNA'S 3:2:1 RECIPE

It's not uncommon to be left with a glut of vegetables wondering what the hell to do with them. You have boiled, roasted and blanched halfway across the globe and back again, and yet they just keep coming. But there is another way.

Pickling is a proven method of infusing new flavours into old tastes, and more than that, will greatly increase the shelf life of the produce, which can then be put aside for a rainy day. One of the skills of a seasonal eater is making sure bountiful seasons can be revisited when things get bleak, and pickling stinks of good times.

Wrapping your head around the pickling process can sometimes prove troublesome, as recipes and theories are as varied as the colour of your underpants, so we thought it was about time to provide some clarity around our favourite method: Nonna's 3:2:1.

Nonnas are masters in the art of preserving, but not skilled in the idea of following recipes. Our first attempts to etch out Nonna's 3:2:1 were foiled by measurements as accurate as 'ah abouta dat much!' or 'ita dependza', but we finally ground her down and have painted a clearer picture.

The most important thing about preserving is keeping a sterile environment. Remember, you're preparing food that is about to get bottled up, hopefully for a very long time, and anything funky that you introduce now will only intensify in funkiness. You're preserving history here and it's a responsibility you need to take seriously. Only then will you realise that some things truly do get better with age.

Before starting with the produce, **STERILISE** your jars by boiling them in a large saucepan of water for a few minutes. Having a sterile environment is very important for food that will be kept over the weeks, months and potentially years ahead.

< **1**

Now, **PREPARE** the produce - big bold beetroots in this case - by rinsing and halving them. Smaller beets can be kept whole, but when dealing with larger specimens that have gone a little wild, they will need to be halved or even quartered so they cook more evenly.

2 >

Pop the beetroot pieces in some boiling water in the large saucepan and cook for about 10-15 minutes over medium heat.

< **3**

>>

As they bubble away, prepare the **PICKLING MIXTURE**. Remember that you will need enough liquid to cover the produce in the jars. Rather than getting precise by subtracting the volume of the individual beetroot from the volumes of the jar (confused already, aren't you?), just make enough mixture to fill the empty jars. We used 3 cups of water, 2 cups of white-wine vinegar and 1 cup of sugar (and a pinch of salt).

‹ 4

Boil the pickling mixture in a saucepan for 5 minutes or until the sugar is dissolved. Continuously stir as the mixture heats to avoid burning the sugar. If you need more pickling mixture, you can change the quantities but you must stick to the 3:2:1 ratio.

5 ›

‹ 6

Check to see if the beetroot's ready. The pieces should be soft enough for a knife to easily pierce the skin, but meet some resistance when the point of the blade enters the centre. It's nice to retain some **TEXTURE**. The worst result is a pile of mashed beetroot, so err on the side of caution. When in doubt, undercook.

‹ 7

Rinse the beetroot chunks under some cold water and rub the skins off with your thumbs. This saves you peeling them prior to cooking and any potential staining of the granite benchtop that maybe wasn't sealed properly. For Nonna, the taste of these pickles is equally as important as a well-kept kitchen.

Pass the pieces through a mandoline or for those looking to test their **KNIFE SKILLS**, cut with a large, sharp blade to no more than 2–3 mm thick. You may joke that if you cut your finger there would be no way of distinguishing beetroot juice from the blood. There really wouldn't …

8 ›

‹ 9

Now it's time to **INFUSE** your flavours and really 'make' the pickled beetroot by preparing your jars with the spices. For each 500 ml (17 fl oz/2 cups) jar, we throw in a tablespoon of coriander seeds and the same of mustard seeds, 4–5 cloves and a couple of good pieces of lemon rind.

»

< 10 Add the sliced beetroot and then top up with the warm pickling juice to within a finger of the top of the jar.

Seal tightly with a lid and record the vintage as well as the types of spices you used. We called this one 'Nonna's 3:2:1'.

11 >

12 Flipping the jars over until the liquid cools down will help to make an airtight seal.

13

Over time the pickling mixture will gradually pick off the flavour from the spices and push it though the beetroot. The longer they are allowed to do this, the **TASTIER** the pickles are going to be, so best to be patient and let them weave their magic in a cool, dark place for at least 2 weeks before opening. Refrigerate after your first helping.

PROJECT DETAILS

TIME 🕐 🕐 🕐

DIFFICULTY RATING

BUDGET 💲①

THINGS YOU'LL NEED...

- 45 g (1½ oz/¼ cup) organic whole green lentils
- large quart-sized canning jar with lid
- water
- cheesecloth (or sprouting screen)
- medium bowl
- storage container

GROWING SPROUTS

KEEPING THE KITCHEN FULL OF CRUNCH

During the cold, dark months of winter it's easy to fall into a pattern of comfort. The body craves hearty meals, and vegetables are readily abundant in the garden and pantry. Brassicas and root vegetables fill the patch, while the larder is stocked with pumpkin and potatoes, foods that warm and nourish us through the cold season. At this time of year, freshness can be hard to come by, particularly if you're trying to eat what's in season.

Sprouting has become a favourite solution for a little winter freshness, but doesn't have to be limited to winter. Much like marinated goat's cheese, sprouts never go out of season and should be enjoyed year-round. Unlike marinated goat's cheese, however, the health benefits of sprouts are tremendous and well documented. They are easy to digest and packed with proteins, vitamins, minerals and amino acids.

Like so many things in the culinary world, you can get lost in an abundance of products. There are some great sprouting mixes out there and plenty of cool toys, but I generally try to follow the KISS method – that is, Keep It Simple Stupid. The rule of thumb seems to be that the bigger the seed, the easier it is to sprout. A great place to start is lentils, as they are easy to find and readily available just about everywhere on the planet.

1 Pour the lentils into the canning jar and add about 2 cups of water. Any old packet of lentils will do provided that they are 'whole'.

Cut a piece of cheesecloth and cover the mouth of the jar. The real pros use a 'sprouting screen', which works the same as cheesecloth but is harder to come by. **SECURE IN PLACE** by screwing on the lid. If you don't have access to a canning lid or cheesecloth, just use a fine sieve to strain the water.

2

3 **SWIRL** the water around to rinse the lentils, much like washing rice. Dump the water out – it should drain right through the cloth – and repeat the rinsing and draining one more time.

After the second rinse, fill the jar with water again. Store the jar overnight. The next morning, dump the water out, rinse and drain the lentils.

Once the lentils are well drained, turn the jar upside down and rest it in a bowl that will allow the jar to remain at a slight angle. Continue this process of rinsing and draining each morning and evening, ensuring you drain any built-up water from the bowl.

5 ›

‹ 6

Sprouts will start to form in a matter of days, and will be **EDIBLE** immediately. Just how long you let them grow is a matter of taste and patience.

‹ 7

Once you are satisfied with the growth, empty the sprouts onto a dry paper towel. Lightly pat the batch with the paper to absorb any extra moisture.

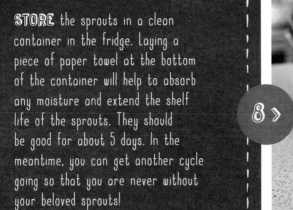

STORE the sprouts in a clean container in the fridge. Laying a piece of paper towel at the bottom of the container will help to absorb any moisture and extend the shelf life of the sprouts. They should be good for about 5 days. In the meantime, you can get another cycle going so that you are never without your beloved sprouts!

8 ›

Enjoy as a **TASTY** complement to any meal. Or, perhaps, just eat them by the handful while silently crying in the bathtub.

PROJECT DETAILS

TIME

DIFFICULTY RATING

BUDGET

THINGS YOU'LL NEED...

- seeds
- propagating tray
- seed raising mix
- hose or water spray bottle
- mini greenhouse (if growing in winter)
- scissors

GROWING MICRO HERBS

CLASSIC COOKING

If you're in the habit of angling for compliments when preparing meals in the kitchen, it's important to constantly refine and expand your culinary repertoire. Any home chef knows that kind words dry up quickly when cooking gets stale, and the only way to keep wooing your guests is to keep abreast of emerging trends. Unfortunately, this has become more difficult since *Iron Chef* funding was cut back in 1999, but one style that is still in vogue is the micro herb.

We still get customers coming into the store asking to purchase micro herb seeds, unaware that they are just basic seeds harvested at an early age. Rather than rub their faces in their shocking ignorance, we hand over the seeds of choice and it is then their responsibility to grow only to micro size.

A micro herb – or micro green – is any herb or leafy green that is harvested no less than a few weeks after germination. Rather than possessing the stronger flavour of a mature herb or vegetable, the taste of a micro green is more refined and subtle. When this is combined with the delicate texture of the young seedling, you then have a powerful culinary tool.

Growing micro herbs is dead easy. Choose your variety, propagate them, and once the seedlings have germinated and developed their first true set of leaves, they are ready to be harvested. Taken so young, micro herbs seem mostly immune from the pest and disease problems more prevalent with mature produce. There is not even the need to thin them out. Once they get to that stage, you will find yourself harvesting them anyway.

1

There are a number of varieties that are well suited to be grown as micro herbs and, ironically, not many of them are herbs – rather, they are **GREENS**. These include mustard, chicory (endive), tatsoi, radish, watercress, spinach, peas, cabbage and basil. A combination of flavour and speed of germination make these good choices.

‹ 2

Fill the propagating tray with seed raising mix. This drains even more freely than standard potting mix as it contains a sprinkling of sand through it. This is important, as the seeds will receive frequent watering.

Growing micro herbs involves the same approach as propagating any seed. Sow seeds at a depth of half their diameter. You don't need to be regimented about the spacing of the seeds, as they will all manage to get to micro herb stage without any real impediment. If planting during winter, use the mini greenhouse. Position it outside in the sunshine during the day, and bring it inside at night.

‹3

After sowing, the main responsibility is to keep the mix damp, without soaking it. Use the hose or a water spray bottle to give your plants frequent, short waterings a couple of times a day.

4›

‹5

Once the seeds have germinated, we wait until the seedling produces two true leaves, usually within 2–3 weeks. The first leaves that sprout are, in fact, baby leaves that soon shed. These are quite different in appearance to the next set that marks **MATURITY** as a micro green.

6

Once the **TRUE LEAVES** appear, you can use scissors to harvest the micro greens.

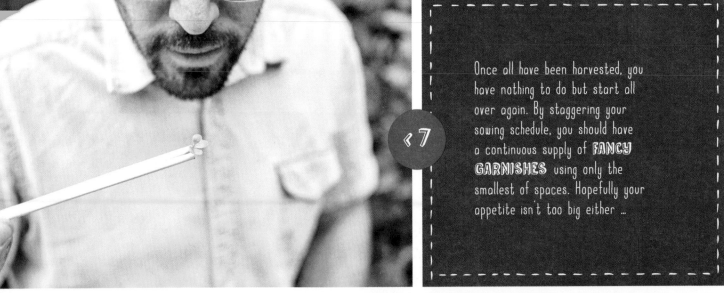

‹7

Once all have been harvested, you have nothing to do but start all over again. By staggering your sowing schedule, you should have a continuous supply of **FANCY GARNISHES** using only the smallest of spaces. Hopefully your appetite isn't too big either ...

PROJECT DETAILS

TIME

DIFFICULTY RATING

BUDGET

THINGS YOU'LL NEED...

- little helpers
- 250 g (9 oz) strawberries
- any other fresh berry you can find!
- 2 large handfuls mint, leaves picked
- 2 large handfuls stevia, leaves picked (optional)
- 2 x saucepans
- 2 litres (68 fl oz/8 cups) water
- colander or strainer
- icy pole moulds

Note: Stevia is simple to grow and makes a lovely, natural sweet additive. However, it's not an essential ingredient, and you can easily leave it out for this recipe.

MAKING NATURAL ICY POLES
TREATS WITHOUT TANTRUMS

Icy pole (popsicle, ice lolly) was about the fourth word my child Emiliana learnt. Ice cream was third. Mama was second. And I think it's pretty obvious what was first ...

The fact that icy pole was part of my child's vocabulary well before things like Nonna, Buppa (a mispronunciation of Grandpa), even food and water, shows just how important an icy pole is in a child's life. It is something they will quickly become familiar with – and you, as a parent or aunty or uncle or friend, will have to get accustomed to fast.

Every parent knows the power of the icy pole. It is a valuable commodity. It can smooth over even the most diabolical of situations. It's a 'get out of jail free' card of sorts, but not one without cost. The power of an icy pole is similar to that of a saltwater crocodile. Its obvious strength is at the front end, but just when you think you're past it, it has a tail and a wallop that can be just as earth-shattering. And that's like your child dealing with the post-sugar jitters.

The beauty and beast of a traditional icy pole is the sugar within it. For a child, sugar is their substance of dependency. It's what gets them so pumped for the icy pole. But the come-down is a thing of legend.

By using natural ingredients, grown and harvested from your patch, you can create icy poles that are full of goodness from start to finish.

< 1

Gather your little helpers. We're going on a food hunt. For this mission, we are after strawberries, mint and stevia. To ensure there are strawberries available for the icy poles, perhaps pick enough before the mission. Everyone knows that kids get **SLIPPERY FINGERS** around strawberry bushes.

Gather the ingredients together in a well-styled and impressive display. Should anybody walk by they will know that you mean business.

2 >

3

Hull the strawberries and cut them into quarters.

>>

< 4

Chop up the stevia and mint roughly, throw them into a saucepan with the water and place over high heat until you bring it to the boil. **SIMMER** for 5–10 minutes. Boiling the stevia helps to release the natural sugars from the leaves, which can then be used to cook the strawberries. The mint will also infuse the mix, leaving its mark.

5

Put your strawberries into another saucepan and strain the stevia and mint liquid over the top.

< 6

Cook over low heat for about 15–20 minutes, ensuring you keep the liquid moving. This is the icy pole mixture – you're now face to face with it! It should reduce down to about half the original volume – roughly 1 litre (34 fl oz/ 4 cups). Remove from the heat and let the mixture cool down before pouring it into the moulds. That way your helpers can be more involved in the process.

‹ 7

Once the mixture is cool enough to handle, pour it into the **MOULDS**. There will still be a good amount of residue lingering in the saucepan so take the opportunity to let your helpers clean up.

Now, transfer the moulds to the freezer and leave overnight. Soon you will be fully stocked with **NATURAL, TASTY ICY POLES**, powerful enough to counter any threat that comes your way.

8 ›

‹ 9

Icy poles are best enjoyed while wearing only the freshest urban attire.

PROJECT DETAILS

TIME

DIFFICULTY RATING

BUDGET

THINGS YOU'LL NEED...

- 500 g (1 lb 2 oz) strawberries (or any ripe, soft fruit)
- 2 medium mixing bowls
- 440 g (15½ oz/2 cups) sugar
- plastic wrap
- cheesecloth or sieve
- spoon
- 500 ml (17 fl oz/2 cups) balsamic vinegar
- whisk
- glass container with lid
- funnel (if needed)

SIPPING VINEGARS (SHRUB)

PRESERVING OLD SUMMER FAVOURITES

From time to time I like to check in with mates in the USA to learn about what is trending on their side of the world. They often paint pictures of pure fantasy like fast internet, electric cars or wearable technologies. I know science fiction when I hear it, but I humour them nonetheless. However, Portland and Seattle do seem to be leading the charge in gastro-trends. These are generally not new revelations but rather the unearthing and relearning of old skills. Everyone seems to be a butcher, brewer or distiller these days, as 18th-century professions are experiencing a resurgence in popularity. Naturally, it was from a Seattle friend that I first heard about sipping vinegars – or shrubs as they are commonly known.

Shrub is a sweetened vinegar-based fruit syrup that was at the peak of its popularity in 18th-century colonial America and England. At the time it was one of the only ways to preserve summer flavours deep into the winter months. Sadly, it fell out of favour with the advent of domestic refrigeration and fruit syrups. Unlike cordials, vinegar is used as an alternative to citrus juices in the preservation process. The end result is a strongly concentrated flavour, with tartness from the vinegar balanced by the sweetness of the sugar.

Back in the day, shrub was used to add strong flavours to cocktails and soda water. Today ... well ... it still tastes really good in cocktails and soda water. The true art is in finding the right combination of ingredients. Though shrub has three simple components (vinegar, fruit and sugar), there are endless variations to experiment with. There's black cherry and balsamic vinegar; cucumber, mint and white-wine vinegar; or strawberry, black pepper and red-wine vinegar. But before you make it too complicated, why not start on the most basic recipe and refine your flavours from there.

‹ 1

Select and wash your fruit of choice. **GOBBLING** a couple of samples is an important part of the selection process. Assemble your **CAST OF CHARACTERS**. Crush soft berries with your hand, or quarter and pit larger pieces of fruit such as strawberries or stone fruit.

2

Put the fruit into the mixing bowl and **STIR** in the sugar, making sure that every piece of fruit is coated.

3

Cover the bowl with plastic wrap and put in the fridge. Over the next couple of days, the sugar will draw liquids from the fruit.

‹ 4

Once the mixture looks like a **CHUNKY** syrup it is ready to be strained. Line a clean mixing bowl with cheesecloth and pour the mixture into the bowl.

〈5 Pull the cheesecloth together and squeeze it to expel as much **SYRUP** as possible into the clean mixing bowl. You will know that you are finished once you can't draw any more syrup from the bundle.

6 Scrape any remaining sugar stuck to the bottom of the bowl into the new mixture.

〈7 Add your vinegar of choice to the mixture. In this case we have chosen to use balsamic. Try to pair the type of fruit with a suitable vinegar flavour. **WHISK** the fruit syrup and vinegar mixture together until all of the sugar is dissolved.

‹ 8

Pour the mixture into a clean glass container (use a funnel if you need to) and put on the lid. Shake the mixture and put it in the fridge.

Periodically check on the container to see if any sediment is accumulating at the bottom. If so, simply give it a **VIGOROUS SHAKE**. Eventually the acids in the juice and vinegar will completely dissolve the sugar.

9 ›

‹ 10

Shrub can be used right away, but will greatly **IMPROVE WITH TIME**. Try it every week and see what tastes best to you. The flavour is strong, so a couple of drops in your drink will go a long way. Shrub will keep in the fridge for up to 6 months if stored properly (with a tight seal).

TOP 5

OF THE PRESERVING WORLD

While it is hard to hold on to a lover's kiss or the perfect summer day, preserving is like a time capsule that can help unite the fruitful past with a bountiful present that helps you to create new memories. It is a method of extending seasonal flavours deep into the leaner months and also a great way to deal with a glut of produce. As long as people have been eating, people have been preserving and this is our top five.

1 PICKLING

This used to seem like a really big challenge to me until I realised just how little goes into the process. Almost anything can be pickled and all of it should be. Start with a basic pickling recipe of sugar, vinegar, water and salt, and then let your ideas run wild. Far from limiting a process, having just a few ingredients gives you the opportunity to fine-tune the levels. Get the basics right and then begin playing with the levels. Try a pickle with a little more sugar, or experiment with different combinations of spices. From cardamon and cloves to mustard and peppercorns, you simply can't go wrong with a pickle, so don't be afraid to get freaky.

No doubt this is the original preserving method, and one that could very well have come about by accident. Urg of the Cave Bear Clan probably left the mushrooms out in the sun for too long, only to discover that they were suddenly lighter and still just as tasty. Not much has changed since then other than the fact that most of us have less body hair and there are a few more products on the market to expedite the process. Whether you use an old window screen in the sun or an elaborate dehydrator, drying is one of the best ways to not only preserve meats and produce, but also get more out of foods that you are already eating. A great example of this is nuts and seeds, which are far more digestible when they have been soaked and dehydrated. That's right, go nuts!

2 DRYING/ DEHYDRATING

This unequivocal champion of the fermentation world manifests itself in various forms all over the planet, and is loved for both its ease of preparation and delicious taste. For explorers of centuries past, sauerkraut was the only produce that they had on long journeys and it was the main way to prevent scurvy at sea. While most of us are no longer concerned with scurvy, we can all benefit from a bit of probiotic bacteria, like that found in yoghurt, which sauerkraut has in abundance. To make the most basic kraut, you need only combine shredded cabbage and salt in a mason jar. The salt will draw liquids from the cabbage and bacteria present in its leaves, and will begin the process of lacto-fermentation. It is safe, reliable, healthy and, above all else, tasty.

5

SUGO

3

JAM

Fruit is absolutely begging to be preserved, and making jam is the best way to do it. Not only is homemade jam a great inclusion in the fridge, but it's also one of the best gifts going around. Wrap a nice bow around the jar and let the praise start rolling in. While you're at it, wrap a nice bow around yourself, too. What a catch! Jam has a universal appeal and it is yet another simple preserve, requiring nothing more than produce, sugar and lemon juice. It is the best way to carry the summer's sweetness through the year and a critical component to the morning routine. Furthermore, jam has long been credited for its influence on music; after all, the Beatles are said to have had hundreds of jam sessions before finally writing the White Album.

4

SAUERKRAUT

Sugo day is the biggest day on our produce calendar, and a preserve that is so much more than a bottle of tomatoes. While the recipe is simple – tomatoes, basil and a few pinches of things – there is a bit more technology at play than the standard preserve. Specifically you will need a bottling machine and a 'tricka-trucka' – that is, a mechanical de-seeding and skinning device that consumes boiled tomatoes and spits out luscious red sauce. Minor equipment aside, sugo is as much about the process as it is the end product. Nothing unites friends and family like a sugo day, and nothing feels more like summer than watching Nonna wield a wooden spoon like a sceptre as she tucks into her fifth glass of rose, all before 11am.

ACKNOWLEDGEMENTS

So many thanks to the wonderful people at Hardie Grant – Hannah Koelmeyer, Mark Campbell, Lucy Heaver, Todd Rechner and Paul McNally – thank you for keeping us on task and putting up with our constant additions and changes. Thank you for gently nudging us away from bad ideas and letting the good ones thrive. We are excited about this new relationship and are looking forward to a long, committed and loving future together. All of us. Together. Forever. Except for Paul.

Special thanks to Hannah Koelmeyer who is equally adept at sculpting vegetables as she is books. Neither of which would have been possible or looked so good without her discerning vision.

To photographer John Laurie for telling the story and absolutely nailing it the first time, every time. And Tom, our workplace inspector, soil site analyst, whatever; you wore that badge and you wore it with pride.

To design guru Kate Barraclough for making what could have been a very dry book about gardens, tools and materials look like something fun and approachable.

To our beloved illustrator Maxine Chaplin, you consistently rescue our ideas where words fall short and somehow make power tools look like something worthy of a cuddle.

- - - - -

A very special thanks to Susie Ashworth, for your supernatural attention to detail and screw sizes. Thank you for making sense of our words and showing us patience that we probably did not deserve.

A special thanks to Rob and Fred of Foodqube (www.foodqube.com.au) with all their help on our half-finished aquaponics system. If anyone wants to meet some legitimately handy people and see the food-growing systems they create, please look them up!

Thanks to Jesse Arneson for always having his finger on the culinary pulse.

To the Kennon family, for providing us with a perfect venue to write this book.

To Tasmania for being a constant source of inspiration and fish.

To the Heslop clan – Elise for lending us your boys and not minding if they come back with a few extra band aids. Charlie and Sam – for being such good sports throughout the photography and your willingness to take on any activity that we threw you into.

And to Emi and Marlowe, for being so wonderful. Emi you are big and your little sister knows it.

INDEX

- - - - -

PROJECT RATINGS

TIME: Time is relative, especially when you're in the midst of creating something truly great!

 "Just leave me alone for a minute!" under 1 hour

"I'm not feeling well, you go with your friends..." 2-3 hours

"I've booked you and the kids in with my parents for the weekend, it's going to be great!" 1-2 days or more

BUDGET: Not only are we your projects leaders but your financial advisors too. Time to grow up, friends. Let's crunch some numbers.

 "I don't get out of bed for anything less." under $20

"Totally worth it." $20–$100

 "Don't let cost get in the way of a great project..." $100 upwards

DIFFICULTY: We all come into this with different talents and whether or not you can drill a straight leader hole or finesse a circle through a square will have some effect on your ability to master these projects from the start.

 "A piece of cake, with a cherry on top."

"A whole cake; no cherries."

"Circles into squares; plenty of finessing; best not to show anyone how this is done, just show them the end result."

This edition published in 2016 by Hardie Grant Books

First published in 2015

Hardie Grant Books (Australia)
Ground Floor, Building 1
658 Church Street
Richmond, Victoria 3121
www.hardiegrant.com.au

Hardie Grant Books (UK)
5th & 6th Floors
52–54 Southwark Street
London SE1 1UN
www.hardiegrant.co.uk

A Cataloguing-in-Publication entry is available from the catalogue of the National Library of Australia at www.nla.gov.au

The Little Veggie Patch Co. DIY Garden Projects
9781743790991

Publishing Director: Paul McNally
Project Editor: Hannah Koelmeyer
Editor: Susie Ashworth
Design Manager: Mark Campbell
Designer: Kate Barraclough
Illustrator: Maxine Chaplin
Photographer: John Laurie
Production Manager: Todd Rechner

Colour reproduction by Splitting Image Colour Studio
Printed in China by 1010 Printing International Limited